TECHNOLOGY DEVELOPMENT HOW ENCOURAGES

SPACE TOURISM

JOHN LOK

Introduction

I shall apply psychology methods to attempt to predict space tourism planner individual space tourism desire in whole future space tourism leisure market development. Whether will future space tourism market development be popular to be accepted one kind of travelling leisure to any travelling consumers in global? What factors can influence traveler prefer to choose space tourism entertainment more than general Earth tourism entertainment? How to influence future space tourism traveler individual space travel entertainment desire to be more stronger? How to attract travelers to feel space tourism entertainment which is one kind of real meaning of life travel leisure at least one time spending? What factors will raise space tourism leisure desire to space travelling planners? How to solve any challenges to raise space travelling planner individual space travel leisure desire?Whether economic environment changing and space tourism leisure facilities and trip planning both factors are the most influential space tourism planner individual leisure consumption desire?

What are the difference traveller psychology between space and earth tourism? In this book, I shall follow travel psychologists and space tourism entertainment businessmen support view points to give my opinions to attempt to answer above questions. My readers will learn how to apply new space travel strategic knowledge to solve and predict future space tourism leisure consumer behavior more accurately.Therefore, it brings these questions: How any why traveller individual travelling choice won't be influenced by travelling entertainment service price only? Does it mean the travelling entertainment service providers will not reduce their traveller number when they can respect or consider above factors to avoid to bring negative influence to traveller consumers, but they still change higher travelling entertainment arrangement service fee to them? In my this part, I shall explain above factors how to influence traveller individual behavior to let readers can predict traveller individual behavior more accurately.
I write this book to aim to give my opinions to let readers to feel how operate or manage one space exploration organization in success.I shall indicate these different factors which influence one successful space exploration successfully. Such as effective organization culture and communication factor, management team and strategy factor, space flight safe factor etc. It is suitable to any readers who pursue to know how manage or operate one space exploration organization in success.

Contents

Prologue

Content of contents

Chapter 1 Psychology and economic environment how influences space tourism development

● Psychology and economic environment changing both factors influence whole space tourism market leisure desire p.5-25

● space tourism strategy

(1) safe space tourism journey

(2) reduction cost expense plan

(3) achieve any space tourism mission plan

Methods to raise space traveler number

● What is the prediction space travelling passenger desire method ?

● The prediction of price factor influences space traveler number

Chapter 2

What are space traveler individual space tourism leisure need p.26-44

● Raising space tourism leisure traveler individual leisure need consumption strategies

Research how to raise space traveler individual leisure desire

Chapter 3

Space travel marketing strategy

p.45-65

(1) On concept of spacecraft design aspect

● Outsourcing spacecraft concept design strategy

(2) On deciding misson aspect

(4) On target audience prediction aspect

(3) On space tourism leisure organization managment aspect

(5) On space objective aspect

● Space tourism leisure behavioral economic consumption model

(1) Economic environment variable factor

(2) Space tourism leisure journey management factor

● Space tourism market moral ethic risk
threats

(1) Potential accidents aspect
(2) Space tourism destinations and space tourism entertainment facilities
safe arrangement challenges aspect
(3) Space tourism market competition challenge aspect
● Can space tourism business bring
economy benefits

(1) On space resource benefit aspect
(2) On education benefit aspect
● What are the tangible social and economic benefits brought from space
tourism?
Chapter 4
Space Tourism Organization Strategy

● Space flight safe factor p.66-86
● Space exploration
organization mission and strategy
● Space exploration
organization communication strategy
● Space exploration organization's human space
life science factor
● What is human space life science strategy?
● How can human space life science strategy implement?
● Situation analysis
What are space life science
strategy goals?
Health innovation goal
Prediction on future trends in
human space flight and future space human life science strategy
relationship.
Why does Japan space
organization consider space
human life science?

Chapter 5

development?
Will technology development influences space tourism needs increase?

Psychology and economic environment how influences space tourism development

● Psychology and economic environment changing both factors influence whole space tourism market leisure desire

How can psychology method predict space tourism leisure desire? I believe that it has relationship between the space tourism planner and the economic environment as well as his/her psychology as below:

Firstly, on the economic environment influence hand, it includs these both economic situations, either in the good economic environment, many people can earn high income and employers can supply many job number to provide to many people to work, then it will influence the space travelling planner has more space travelling desire. Otherwise, or in the bad economic, less people can earn high income and employers can not supply many job number to provide to many people to work, it will influence the space travelling planner has less space travelling desire.

Secondly, on these both the space travelling planner individual psychology influence hand, the space travelling planner will have these both aspects of individual psychological influence, it includes these both either positive or negative psychological influence aspectsas below:

On the positive psychological influence aspect, if the space travelling planner has confidence to the space travelling leisure company can provide safe, comfortable, good quality of one space travelling trip arrangement, good taste food arrangement, reasonable space ticket price and every reasonable space trip for space hotel living arrangement and space garden and space farming land visiting journey arrangement, even, space swimming pool and space sport centre and space cinema leisure arrangement to let whom to stay on the planet at least one day trip, it means not one short time space trip, e.g. the spacecraft only flies about half hour or one half. It can not fly to the planet to arrive its space station destination to stay to let the space travelling planner to live at the space hotel at least one night. Then the space travelling planner will have more desire to choose to catch the space tourism leisure company's spacecraft to travel to space.

Otherwise, on the negative psychological influence aspect, if the space travelling planner lacks confidence to the space travelling leisure company can provide safe, comfortable, good quality of one space travelling trip arrangement, good taste food arrangement, reasonable space ticket price and every reasonable space trip for space hotel living arrangement and space garden and space farming land visiting journey arrangement, even, space swimming pool and space sport centre and space cinema leisure arrangement to let whom to stay on the planet at least one day trip, it means not one short time space trip, e.g. the spacecraft only flies about half hour or one half. It can not fly to the planet to arrive its space station destination to stay to let the space travelling planner to live at the space hotel at least one night. Then the space travelling planner will have less desire to choose to catch the space tourism leisure company's spacecraft to travel to space.

Hence, it seems economic environment changing factor and the space travelling planner's confidence factor to the space tourism leisure providers will influence the whole space travelling market whose space travelling consumer's space travelling leisure consumption desire to be more or less. So, any one space tourism provider can not neglect these both factors how to influence whose customer consumption desire.

● space tourism strategy

Future any space tourism leisure business needs have good business plan to outline the space tourism leisure business in these aspects , such as: different space tourism destinations of every space tourism journey, technical , financial and regulatory factors for growing space tourism leisure consumption into any one kind of unique artificial intelligent space tourism journey for identified passenger target group.

All how to design one space tourism business development plan to attempt to predict whether what trends will influence how every different kinds of identified space tourism journey in order to achieve passenger number growing aim as well as how to achieve one attractive space tourism leisure to satisfy future space tourism passenger individual space travel needs more easily.

I shall indicate what aspects to future every space tourism traveler who will consider in order to reduce the space tourism traveler personal worry to catch any pace boats to leave our Earth to fly to other planets to travel.

I recommend that any space tourism leisure organizations need to concern these aspects in their space tourism leisure business plan as below:

(1) safe space tourism journey

On first aspect concerns safe space tourism journey plan to let all space tourism travelers will considerate safe issue. They must ensure space boats that is safe to catch them to fly to planets in their space journeys. So, any space tourism leisure business will utilize previous flight rated and proven technologies to form the basis for manufacturing spacecraft vehicles, and will incorporate the latest modern avionics and flight systems for ensuring safety, reliability and economical operation in order to reduce any space tourism traveler personal worry to catch any spacecraft.

So, the space tourism safe journey plan is one very important factor to influence space tourism consumer number for them if any one of space tourism leisure business hoped they can grow the space tourism consumer number for long term. For example, the space boat flight hardware must often be maintained at the space station. It is needed to be considered by space boat experts as risky, extremely expensive and potentially sensitive. To aims to ensure spacecraft will offer an economical and safe alternative for any satellite manufacturers and other space tourism entertainment organizations have a desire or requirement for space tourism flight.

(2) reduction cost expense plan

On second aspect concerns reduction cost expense plan, any space tourism entertainment organizations need have the experience and capacity for safely launching a fully loaded , including space tourism passengers and passenger individual cargo for every spacecraft tourism journey. As a result of outsourcing the launch role to a major contractor, the space tourism pilot can concentrate on space boat crews flight training, planning space tourism passenger cargo capacity and preparing space flight manifests , and will as a result, avoid the expense of maintaining a launch operation on a daily basis. In addition, by outsourcing the spacecraft manufacturing, it can avoid spending millions of dollar on facilities and equipment infrastructure and engineering manufacturing expertise.

(3) achieve any space tourism mission plan

On third aspect concerns how to achieve any space tourism mission. Every space tourism mission must be ensure that reliable service is provided to satisfy every space tourism passenger personal space traveler needs and let them to enjoy in their whole space tourism journey, let them to catch a big aircraft in comfortable environment of technologically sophisticated space boat, reasonable and competitive every time space tourism flight ticket price plan is developed and properly revised every time space tourism ticket price when performing their assigned every different space tourism journey mission.

Hence, the space tourism leisure company will provide one careful selected space tourism destination , e.g. Mar planet space tourism journey, Moon planet space tourism journey or no any space destination journey, it means that the space craft only needs to fly one circle around between Earth and Moon space journey etc. that are capable of meeting the requirements of travelling into Earth orbit. So, any space tourism journey must emphasize affordability, reliability, safety, customer service and responsiveness in responding to every client's space tourism journey requirements. Hence, any one of space tourism journey must have clear space journey mission and objective to satisfy any space traveler client target needs.

● Methods to raise space
traveler number

Future space tourism will be one kind of new travel leisure market for any new space travel leisure companies to enter this undiscovered market in the beginning. However, how to predict future 10 to 20 years , even more space traveler number that is one important issue to any new space tourism leisure companies.

I think that space tourism leisure companies need to define what kinds of space travel leisure service to be provided to space travelling passengers, however, what age group of space passengers who will be their space travelling target client. For example, their space travel leisure must provide any flight operation that takes one or more passengers beyond the altitude of 100 km and thus into space to let space travelling passengers who have fun, exciting space travelling feeling.

Anyway, for any kind of space tourism (leisure space travel) journey, space tourism leisure company needs anyone to be bring customer satisfaction, it is a plan or predictive methods to measure how to let every space travelling passenger to feel comfortable when they are catching the spacecraft (space flying product) and they can have enjoyable and fun or exciting feeling when they have need providing any space tourism journey, services meet or surpass customer expectations.

Thus, any space tourism leisure company needs to evaluate the degree of every time space tourism journey's customer satisfaction and customer satisfaction is also always evaluated in relationship to the every time ticket price of the space tourism journey. So, the space tourism leisure company will predict the next time of what the space tourism journey of passenger number is more accurate, after it has evaluated what degree of every time space tourism journey's customer satisfaction is. It aims to gather their opinions to find which aspects that they need to revise, e.g. choosing where will be the next time space tourism journey destination, how to improve spacecraft staff's service attitude and performance to serve to their space tourism passengers when they are catching the spacecraft, to evaluate whether the spacecraft can provide comfortable and safe environment to let them to catch in order to let the next time space travelling passengers can feel satisfactory and enjoyable when they are catching the space tourism leisure's spacecraft to fly to anywhere in space.

In general, the expectation of factors space passengers include the following customer value elements, such as below:

- viewing space and the Earth.
- experiencing weightlessness and being able to float freely in zero gravity.
- experiencing pre-flight astronaut training and related sensations.
- communicating from space to significant others.
- being able to discuss the adventure in an informed way.
- having astronaut like documentation and memorabilia.

These objectives need to be combined with, sometimes conflicting constraints, such as guaranteed safe return, limited training time, reasonable comfort, and minimum medical restrictions. All these above issues which will be every space travelling passenger considerate matters before they choose the space tourism leisure company to catch its spacecraft to fly to space. So, all these factors will influence the next time space passenger number. Any space tourism leisure company can not neglect how to solve these all matters before they decide when their next time space tourism journey to be achieved.

Consequently, if the space craft tourism leisure company could revise what aspects of its last space tourism journey to find what are its wrong or weakness or unattractive challenges to cause any one space travelling passenger who feels unsatisfactory. Then, it can have more effort to concentrate on improving its next space tourism journey to raise its space tourism service performance level , e.g. people, food, leisure etc. service aspects and its space tourism product quality level, e.g. proving comfortable spacecraft facilities to let space travelling passengers to catch in whole spacecraft tourism journey. Then, it will have more confidence to achieve the raising space travelling passenger number.

● What is the prediction space travelling passenger desire method ?

The prediction space travelling passenger individual desire method can be one survey investigation method. When every time spacecraft finishes space tourism journey mission, after all space tourism passengers catch the spacecraft to arrive earth from space. When they arrive earth space station destination, then the space tourism leisure company can arrange survey investigation staffs to enquire their feeling for this time space tourism journey immediately.

The survey content can include as below:

Do you feel satisfactory or unsatisfactory to which aspects of this time space tourism journey?

(1) On service aspect questions include as below:

(a) Do you feel space food taste is good?

(b) Do you enjoy this time space tourism journey arrangement?

(c) Do you feel satisfactory to space staff
service performance?

(d) If you have unsatisfactory feeling for any one of above questions, which aspect issue cause you feel unsatisfactory to explain to let us to know in order to us to revise our service performance.

(2) On product aspect questions include as below:

(a) Do you feel comfortable when you are catching our spacecraft in whole space tourism journey?

(b) If you feel comfortable , may you explain the reasons what aspects of our spacecraft has weakness to cause you feel uncomfortable?

(c) Do you feel safe when you are catching our spacecraft in whole space tourism journey?

(d) If you feel unsafe, may you explain the reasons what aspects of our spacecraft has weakness to cause you feel unsafe?

Finally, we thank your ideas to be given to let us know how to improve our every time future space tourism journey in order to find what challenge cause our service performance and product quality which can not satisfy your needs. So, we shall improve to avoid future challenges continue occur. Our mission is achievement of 100% satisfactory level to our every space travelling passenger individual feeling. Also, we hope that you can choose our space tourism leisure service again, when you have another time space tourism leisure desire need. However, we shall revise to improve our service performance and product quality to be better, after collecting your ideas from this time survey investigation. I think you spend time to give your ideas from this survey investigation faithfully.

So, survey investigation method will be one important idea gathering tool to help any space tourism leisure company to revise the weaknesses to raise or improve future every time space tourism journey service performance and product quality to achieve raising competitive effort in this new space tourism leisure market.

Hence, survey investigation method will be the best idea gathering method to predict how space travelling passenger emotion or desire need will change in order to achieve the objective of raising every time space tourism journey future space travelling passenger number more easily for every space tourism leisure company.

● The prediction of price factor influences space traveler number

The space tourism leisure organizations indicate the total cost of a trip into space is rapidly coming down from the initial price level of about US$600,000, it is obvious that the space travelling customer base is going to be rather small. Typical customers tend to belong to the top 1% income bracket. They also indicate that the price comes down , it is expected that new space travelling customer groups will enter the space tourism leisure market.

Typical new customers include people in other brackets with one-of-a kind incomes, such as inheritance or business sold. There are indications that those types of customers are becoming interested in spending on an once-in-a lifetime space experience. Therefore, the growth of the space tourism market is highly sensitive to customer satisfaction and how it is communicated through various media.

This will establish the status factors of space tourism and corresponding brand reputation service providers. They also suggest that any operator monitors space travelling customer satisfaction closely, as it will help developing increasingly accurate estimates of how the space tourism leisure market will develop.

Hence, it seems that every time space tourism journey price variable factor will influence the time space tourism of customer individual leisure desire and the space tourism passenger number. For example, the minimum price goal foe a variable space tourism business is currently estimate to be below US$3000-4000/kg for a round -trip depending on variable configuration and operation size. At this price, they estimate that somewhat over 1 % of the high income earners are potential customers.

However, for significant volume growth the longer term goal should be below US$2000/kg for a typical passenger, baggage and supplies. The lower price will probably open space tourism to a broader population, expanding the customer base and altering expectations. beyond this point space tourism will become into a travelling competitive leisure commodity, price competition will ensure and service providers need to rethink their space tourism marketing and branding and price strategies.

I shall also recommend how to attract the potential customers successfully. First, space operators need to pay special attention to the right level of customer services. Second, various preparatory customer operations cost, such as a travel to the launch site, space tourism destination accommodation, pre-flight training, medical check-ups and equipment my add up to between 10 to 15 % of the actual space travel cost. Thurs, solving the right balance between services offered and cost of client operation in order to earn the largest intangible benefits, such as loyalty, confidence, leisure enjoyment, comfortable space travelling journey as well as tangible benefits, such as profit, spacecraft manufacturing facilities, space stations, space hotels , space swimming pools, space gardens, space cinema etc. which are built to similar to earth building facilities to satisfy space travelers' needs.

CHAPTER TWO

What are space traveler individual   space tourism leisure need

Nowadays, our earth is no longer an adventurous enough place for some experienced tourists. Space tourism will be a new sector of adventure tourism, which is in the near future will be fast becoming a new tourism leisure opportunity for experiencing the unknown. Of one day, space tourism is able to reach the mass tourism phase, due to improved safety and decreased operation costs, a future space tourist will possibly only need minimal training to cope with the zero cost.

Space tourism is quite well established with visits to space attraction and launch sites, and it is a wealthy trips to the international space station for any space tourism travelers. However, if any space tourism leisure companies can attempt to find what the most influential factors are to persuade travelers feel attraction more than travelling in our earth.

It aims to let travelers to choose space travelling more than earth travelling when they feel travelling leisure need. I shall indicate what will be the most important influential factors to persuade travelers to choose space tourism more than earth tourism as below:

Firstly, I shall argue that the majority of different new space tourism journey destinations will be needed to find to satisfy different aged space travelers and different income space tourism consumers‘ needs. For example, the rich people have effort to consume longer time and reach any space tourism destinations where are far away from our earth of their every space tourism journey.

Otherwise, the middle income people will choose shorter space tourism journey distance from our earth and short time space tourism journey. Also, younger space tourism clients can accept more longer journey time, exciting fast speed spacecraft flying journey. Otherwise, old space tourism clients can only accept comfortable and shorter time safe space journey. So, it seems that safety, comfortable feeling, shorter time space tourism journey won't be one important influential factor to excite any young people who choose to consume space tourism leisure. Otherwise, safety, comfortable feeling, shorter time space tourism journey will be one important influential factor to excite any old people who choose to consume space tourism leisure.

Secondly, the another most important influential factor to excite space travelers to choose space tourism , it concerns whether the space travelers will feel what tourists benefits can be earned from a substantial variety of destinations choice. In general, space tourism with those of aviation, space travelers will hope space tourism will be travelling distances by air in a very short time, safely and comfortably, to bring them to arrive any space planet destinations when spacecraft reaches any space stations to stay in any space destinations.

Hence, space destination factor will bring important influential choice to any space destination journeys. As a result of the space technological tourism boom, the number of potential different space destination, choice attractions have grown with far fewer places on earth to which human do have access yet. However, the ultimate different space destinations to which many of us dream is not on earth, but as least 100 km above us, anywhere in space any planets.

If the space tourism leisure company can provide different space tourism destination choices to young or old age both space traveler target consumer groups. They will feel a real holiday when they will be able to enjoy a great image of the earth from planets. It might mean that every space tourism journey can provide different space tourism destination to let space travelers have another new travelling destinations where are far from our earth anywhere.

Hence, the different space tourism destinations will give them an unforgettable adventure. Think of how it would be to be able to check in at a " billion strategy" luxury hotel in space one planet, it means that the space planet destination can provide one luxury hotel to let space travelers to live one night or more in the space planet destination, how it would be to schedule the space traveler' vacation at one of the space tourism leisure company luxury resorts on the Moon or Mars.

This images seem from science fiction movies, but one should not forget that 100 years ago, the Wright brothers, aviation pioneers inventors and builders of the air plane, would not have imagined how, every day it is possible that future spacecraft can fly to any planets to let human have chance to stay in the space hotel one night or more.

Consequently, space destination choice and space tourism journey service performance, aviation safety, ticket price and leisure satisfactory feeling which will be important influential factors to attract future space travelers to choose space tourism leisure to replace earth tourism leisure in future one day.

● Raising space tourism leisure
consumption strategies

Although, space tourism industry is a real enjoyment and exciting travelling leisure to human. It is possible that human will choose to consume space tourism leisure to replace earth tourism leisure, if human felt that earth tourism leisure is not attractive to them to consume to go to anywhere to travel in their leisure time.

But, I believe that space tourism industry has still many factors to influence human to choose to consume space tourism leisure, even they will consider space tourism leisure consumption I is only one time space tourism in their life time. Hence, space tourism companies ought achieve this aim to persuade or attract everyone prefer to spend space tourism leisure at least one time in their life, then it can represent success. However, I think to achieve this aim, it has these challenges to influence their success, even they believe space tourism leisure business is one potential attractive travel entertainment business. These challenges include such as: expensive space tourism ticket price issue, catching spacecraft safe issue, space traveler personal body health issue, age issue, family and friend relationship influence issue, working time and holiday time arrangement issue, the space trip arrangement issue, weather issue etc. different challenges, which will have possible to influence every space tourism planner either who decide change to cancel the time space tourism plan, or forgive to choose space tourism leisure in their life forever.

Hence, how to raise space tourism leisure consumption desire will be one considerable matter for any space tourism leisure businessmen. I shall indicate my personal three aspect of strategical opinions to let them to know how to raise every space tourism planner individual space tourism leisure consumption desire to avoid every time space tourism passenger number will have decrease failure chance as below:

● (1) Strategic opinion

On the first aspect of strategic opinion, I feel that the space education tutor can teach new space knowledge to let every space traveler to learn any new space and earth knowledge during he/she is catching on the spacecraft in personal contact learning experience environment which can raise space tourism consumption desire. The reason is because the space tourism leisure traveler can raise extra space and earth learning knowledge when they can catch the spacecraft to fly and contact the space environment to learn and feel what the differences are between space and earth by himself or herself. Hence, it is very attractive to the space traveler student target group and I believe that their parents will encourage their sons or daughters to participate the time of space trip and they are more preferable to help them to buy the time space trip ticket, due to their sons and daughters can learn any space knowledge when they are studying. Moreover, every space traveler will feel surprise to learn any new space and earth knowledge from the space tutor's teaching, due to he/she is unknown that this space travel trip includes learning space and earth knowledge.

I suggest that the space tourism leisure businessmen can give learning opportunity to every travel trip space travelers to feel that this space actual environment can bring what disadvantages or advantages to influence our earth when they are catching aircraft to fly to space to travel in every space trip. The space and earth learning knowledge can include these two aspects of space learning knowledge and experience below:

On the teaching of space environment learning knowledge hand, the topics can include as below:

Firstly the space learning topic can concern how space environment influences water and hydrated minerals change , they can learn what our drinking water function how is applied to space environment. For example, in the space environment, they can learn and attempt to feel that how water can be used in protecting astronauts against harmful radiation from the sun and cosmic rays by cloaking spacecraft with a thin layer of water in the actual space environment as well as the space travelers can also feel water is same as fuel when they are catching the spacecraft, they can feel the water is heavy to transport into space when they are catching the spacecraft to fly to space during their whole space tourism journey.

Moreover, when their spacecraft reaches anyone of planets and it stays on the planet's space station, e.g. Moon space station. They can learn how to attempt to contact the hydrated minerals to learn and feel what they contained in some asteroids may be possible sources of water and fuel in the actual space environment. When they are walking in actual space environment, such as Moon planet, they can contact or touch this hydrated minerals to learn how water molecules can be extracted and separated chemically to produce hydrogen fuel knowledge in the actual space environment. This is one exciting space learning experience to the space travelling student passengers.

Secondly the space learning topic can concern how human fights space threats , even when their whole space leisure journey, the space science teacher can let the space trip student passengers to feel that they are learning new space knowledge between the space science teacher and whose space trip student passengers. Such as how to protect our earth knowledge: Teaching them to know when will be threats to our earth from space. The space science teacher can explain how this space threating environment influences our life safety and let them to feel that a mass extinction can be triggered if an asteroid 10 kilometers across hit the earth. Even being the apex species in the food chain did not space carnivorous dinosaurs from such disaster, who knows if this terrifying scene won't happen before our eyes? So, the space travelers can image and feel how the space threating environment can influence their life safety in the actual space environment as well as the space science teacher can let whose space travelers to feel and image the actual earth disaster will possible happen suddenly to let they feel afraid in the actual space environment. Also the space science teacher can teach how our earth can fright the space stones attack to let the space traveler to know, when an impactor targets an asteroid for a controlled well-times wallop. The collision will change the asteroid's momentum, deflecting it from its original orbital path which intersects with that of the earth. So, at the moment, the space travelers can image they are a larger spacecraft near an asteroid which can also change the path. Given enough time, the gravitational pull from the spacecraft will be able to steer the asteroid away from the earth. So, every space traveler will feel that they are catching the spacecraft in the safe space environment to avoid the Earth disaster from space sudden unpredictable attack.

It is more fun real space tourism knowledge learning feel to let every space traveler has chance to learn any new space science knowledge when he/she is catching the spacecraft to fly to space to travel. Hence, one successful space trip ought include trip and learning experience both contents in order to raise every the space tourism planner individual space trip consumption desire.

● (2) Strategic opinion

On the second aspect of strategic opinion, space tourism leisure companies need to let planning travelers feel that anyone of space tourism leisure is very different to general tourism leisure. In general, tourism leisure is visiting at least one night for leisure and holiday, business or other tourism purposes in Earth only. Otherwise, space tourism leisure is other kind of an unique trip leisure or entertainment method, e.g. the space traveler can catch the spacecraft to visit any planets to stay to live at the planet's space hotel at least one night, e.g. Future potential populated Moon or Mars space hotel space trip. Moreover, the space travel companies ought give chance to let them to feel what weightless feeling is in weightlessness environment when they are walking on Moon or other planets in possible. Even, they can attempt to build these entertainment facilities, instead of space hotels, such as space swimming pools, space gardens, space cinema etc. building facilities. It aims to let them to feel what the differences between Earth and space life when they are walking on the Moon, when they are swimming on the space pools, when they are living in space hotels, when they are watching movies in space cinemas, when they are seeing flowers and different species of planets and fruits. e.g. oranges, apples, bananas, and vegetable and potatoes and tomatoes in space gardens. It is very exciting and fun space trip life experience between one days to seven days. So, they believe that they must not feel these space life experience if they do not choose to participate this time space trip planning journey by the space trip company preparation.

Also, due to that the space tourism passengers need to the pre-flight checks and training before they ensure to qualify to permit to participate the space trip. So space travel companies need to concern how to take care their health check and training matter considerately. It aims to let every space traveler will feel a market segment with fitness and extreme experiences as well as he/she will become popular with a market segment passenger to the space tourism leisure company, although he/she must not guarantee to pass the space training and/or pre-flight health checks to permit to participate the space trip. However, he/she can believe that he/she is one worth space travelling passenger to the space tourism leisure company, even this time pre-flight health check or/and the short time space trip training requirements are failure. However, the space tourism leisure company must need to let all pre-flight health check and space trip training passengers to feel that it is only one space tourism which can give them and let customers view the space travel is as the ultimate showcase for health, even though a majority of the population can pass the pre-flight medical and other tests in order to raise their confidence and safety to catch the spacecraft to fly to space to travel when they are confirmed to pass these tests to permit to catch the spacecraft later.

In general, the expectations of future space passengers include the following customer value elements, such as below:

● Viewing space and the Earth.

● Experiencing weightlessness and experiencing pre-flight astronaut training and related sensations.

● Communicating from space to significant others.

● Being able to discuss the adventure in an informed way.

● Having astronaut-like documentation and memorabilia.

● Enjoying one exciting and fun space trip.

However, instead of considering these objectives need to be combined with, sometimes conflicting , constraints such as guaranteed safe, return , limited training time, reasonable comfort, and minimum medical restrictions. So, space tourism companies need to reduce every space traveler individual worries before they decide to make the time of space tourism journey. Then, it can increase their confidence to raise their space tourism consumption desire more successfully.

Consequently, instead of these consideration, a space travel operator must pay attention to the total customer experience over the entire customer process, starting from how the service is presented, proposed and sold. The service package must include training, instructions, travel to the launch site and various post. Travel activities to generate maximum customer satisfaction and brand building opportunity.

(3) Strategic opinion

On the final aspect of strategic opinion, I think any space tourism companies space tourism companies need to consider every time space tourism ticket price and space tourism trip issues. It is important factor to influence every space traveler individual consumption desire. Due to space trip ticket price must be more expensive to compare common Earth trip travelling ticket price, so this kind of tourism leisure market target customer will be the rich and high income customer group.

On the space trip ticket challenge issue, despite that fact the total cost of a trip into space is rapidly coming down from the initial price level of about US$60,000, it is obvious that the customer base is going to be rather small and the client target customer is only high income or rich consumer group. Typical customers tend to belong to the top of the top 1% income bracket. So, ensures that space traveler number must be less than common Earth traveler number.

Also, such as the space trip ticket price, it is expected that new middle rich level or middle high level income customer target group will enter the space trip leisure market, when every space trip ticket price falls down about 1% Typical new customers include people in other income brackets with one-of-a-kind incomes, such as inheritance or business sold space traveler target group. These people will be space travel new client group, when its every space trip ticket price can be reduced to close 1 to 2 % nearly. If any space tourism leisure companies expect to attract new rich and/or high income target customer group to choose any one kind of space trip journey planning to consume.

These are indications that these types of customers are becoming interested in spending on an once-in-a-lifetime space experience. Therefore, the growth of the space tourism market is highly sensitive to customer satisfaction and how it is communicated through the various media. This will establish the status –factor of space tourism, and corresponding brand reputation of service providers. The minimum price goal for a variable space tourism business is currently estimate to be below US$3-4000/kg for a round-trip depending on vehicle configuration. So, space travel leisure companies need to concern every round space trip cost, it can depend on the space vehicle number and weight issue to influence every space trip ticket price variable to achieve how much it can earn.

On space journey design factor aspect, it includes these different facilities aspects how to design, because future space travelling consumers will concern whether the space travel company can provide special entertainment to satisfy their needs. The facilities include as below:

How to design space hotels to let them to live in comfortable space environment and eat the best taste and fresh food quality when the cookers need to cook in the space hotel in the space environment? How to design space swimming pools to let them to swim in safe space environment? How to design space sport centers to let them to run more easily in one space sport warm and safe environment? How to design one space garden to let them to see different species of Earth flowers, or plants? How to design one space farming land to let them to see different species of Earth fruits, vegetables, tomatoes, potatoes etc. fresh foods growth in warm and safe space farming land environment? How to design one space cinema to let them to watch movies in one safe and warm space cinema environment? All these facilities will be any one of future space trip's' important and attractive space trip leisure facilities to influence every space traveler to choose to buy the space tourism leisure company's space trip leisure service.

Instead of these space building entertainment facilities, they also need to concern how the space vehicle entertainment tools are provided the entertainment service to satisfy their needs. When the space travelers can sit on the space vehicles to move on any planets' lands, such as Moon. A number of space vehicle options exist in the market, mainly differing based on the seat capacity as well as the in-flight experience level offered. The typical space vehicle solution is a small, relatively light weight spacecraft taking between 2 to 10 passengers. The number of passengers depends on the service level, amenities and extra offered. The trip typically lasts about 10 hours and of which about 4 hours are spent in space. The main attraction is the weightless time after in space. The main attraction is the weightless time after re-entry has started. It is a rather low-G technology and therefore the medical requirements for participants are nor very high.

Consequently, the space vehicles, space leisure building facilities, the space trip reasonable price ticket level, every safe space trip journey arrangement, clean and fresh and good taste space food arrangement, space traveler individual real learning experience etc. these factors will be the main influential factors to raise the space tourism leisure company's competitive effort and the space traveler consumer individual consumption desire to the space tourism leisure company in the future.

Research how to raise space traveler individual leisure desire
The first factor may raise space traveler leisure desire is that space rocket needs have safe and clean inside environment. Future, space tourism may be another kind of possible popular tourism leisure activity, because since COVID 19 disease occurs, it may influence many travellers feel afraid to

catch air planes in the high risk closed window airt plane inside environment, when many different countries people must need to body contact or air contact. Hence, it is possible that our tourism leisure will not be popular in our earth, if COVID 19 disease , even other unknown air disease may occur to cause global travellers feel fear to catch air planes to avoid life danger in the one hour, even more than 12 hours sitting air plane flying time. Otherwise, because any space tourism rockets are small and it only allows one to four space travellers and space rocket pilot to sit in the space rockets as well as any space journey is only spent 15 minutes to 30 minutes for view moon space journey or more than one day visiting moon space journey or up to one week visiting space station journey in the space rockets. So, owning COVID 19 disease travellers can permit to sit in the space rocket, the chance is low to get COVID 19 disease when the space rocket has less passengers are sitting in the space rocket. It means that when many space travellers feel any space rocket is safe and clean in the inside none window space rocket environment, this safe and clean space rocket inside environment feeling, it cam emcourage many future space passengers begin to choose to catch any one space rocket to leave earth to fly to space to travel in possible. Hence, when space rocket can be invented to bring equipment safe and comfortable feeling and guarantees none of any one owning COVID 19 disease patient can sit in the space rocket as well as all of they can catch this space rocket to earth and come back to earh safely . It means that any one space tourism leisure service provider can guarantee without any sudden accidents occurrence in space. The another most important factor may be every space tourism can charge reasonable ticket price to any one space trip to let any one space tourism leisure consumer to feel. All of these factors may influence the space tourism leisure consumers number increases to the space tourism leisure service provider.

Instead of above space trip ticket price and space rocket's safe and clean inside environment both aspects. I shall indicate how to raise space traveller individual leisure desire methods as below:

Firstly. attractive space trip is another important factor to influence any one space tourism leisure consumers to choose the space tourism leisure service provider's any one space tourism leisure activities. Because of the space trip's time is short, e.g. 15 minutes to 30 minutes leaving earth to stay on space for viewing our earth leisure , within this 15 to 30 minutes short space trip time, the space tourism leisure service provider needs to seek the different kinds of attractive space destinations to let every space tourism leisure passengers to feel enjoyable in space different locations when they see our earth from their rocket's staying different locations in space. Because different space locations, they can influence different viewing feeling of our earth from the rocket. So, choosing the suitable different space locations to stay in order to view earth , this short time space staying locations trip is very important to influence every passenger whose viewing earth feeling. Otherwise, if the space trip's time is longer, e.g. more than 5 hours sitting to visit moon space trip. The space trip must need to be arrangement have more attractive feeling to let they do not feel boring when they need to sit more than 5 hours in the space rocket to arrive the moon. So, their sitting space rocket times are needed to be feel leisure times for every passenger. They can not feel bore or non space trip arrangement leisure feeliing in the whole space trip. So, when the space trip is longer time, its space leisure activities arrangement ought need have enough different leisure activities to provide in order to avoid any one space passenger feels bore, e.g. spending one week to arrive space station space trip, the rocket must need have sport equipment or cinema provide to let they do not feel bore when they need to sit about one week time to go to the space station as well as spend another one week time to come back earth from the space station. Otherwise, short time space trip , e.g. only 15 minutes viewing earth space trip , it doe not any space trip leisure activities, because this space viewing earth trip aims to let passengers can feel comfortable and enjoyable to view our earth when they are sitting in the rocket in this 15 minutes. However, this rocket needs to fly to about 4 to 5 different space locations to let passengers to feel different viewing earth visable feeling. If the rocket is only staying in one same space location to let them to view our earth. They must feel bore to view the same visable feeling of our earth in this 15 minutes space viewing earh trip. So, space locations choice factor is very important for short time viewing earth space trip. Consequently, they may feel their this short time viewing earth space trip ticket price is unreasonable.

Hence, any one space trip lesiure activities and space staying locations choice arrangement, as well as its space trip time as well as its evaluated ticket price, they must have close relationship to influence any one space trip traveller individual leisure satisfactory feeling in this space tourism leisure development industry. Hence, if any one space tourism leisure service provider hopes that they can have many space travellers to choose their any one long or short time space trip lesisure activities. They must need to consider how to design space trip in order to attract their leisure choices , how to evaluate every space trip's time and space trip ticket price in order to achieve how to attract many future space traveller individual preference space trip choice among potentient different space trip lesisure providers. Because when future space tourism leisure is popular to accept. In this space tourism market, it will have many potential space tourism leisure service providers attempt to anticipate and implement any kinds of space trip leisure activities arrangement, it seems future space trip may influence our traditional tourism industry from earth travel changes to space travel lesisure direction development.

In earth tourism industry, every travel leisure service provider needs to design different kinds of travelling destinations in order to attract different countries travellers choose to play themselves designing trips packages, if their trips arrangements are attrractive, it will influence thr traveller chooses this travel agent's trip to visit the another country service. Hence, earth trip's travelling packages are very important to influence every traveller individual travel agent choice. It seems that space tourism trip arrangement may be another main factor to influence space passengers number increases or decreases to any one space leisure service provider. The question concerns how to design attract space trip to any one space traveller choice preference. I shall explain as below:

IN fact, space tourism's general price is expensive, so the wealthiest people ought be any ones space tourism leisure provider's main customer target. But advances in rocket and capsule design also also expected to lower the price to the point that people of more modest fortunes are able to afford a ticket. What space tourists can expect? What exactly is on store for space tourists? The excitment of a rocket ride and a chance to experience weightlessness for starters. And bragging rights are hard to beat. But some the biggest benefit of point into space is getting a dramatic new outlook on life when any one space traveller can try to catch rocket to leave our earth home.

For Virgin Galactic plans to offer suborbital space trips, with customers being treated to feel of weightlessness feeling. He says more than 600 customers have signed contracts to already to pay a ticket price US$250,000 for one time space trip. Another space tourism leisure provider, e.g. Blue Origin, Amazon CEO Jeff Bezos , thees space tourism leisure providers had begun to plan future space adventures leisures to satisfy future any one space traveller individual space trip leisure need. In general, average a ticket price is between US$75,000 to US$300,000. SO, wealth people must be space travel consumer targert customer.

Future space trip may include: Flying to space stations, it may be a big vacation will be able to buy a rocket ride into orbit, future NASA is not transfoming into a space travel agency, private companies will have to pay it about US$35,000 a night per passenger to sleep in the space station's beds and use its amenities, including air, water , the internet and toilet. Hence, flying to space station may be one attract one to two weeks attractive space trip.

Another kind of space trips, such as a variety of options for private of spaceflight have started to emergy. Virgin Galactic, founded by the entrepreneur Richard Branson, and Blue Origin from Jeffrey P. Benos of Amazon, both plan to carry passengers on short suborbital flights, space X also announced that Yusaka Maezawa, a Japanese, clothing company founder, would pay for a trip around the moon on a spacecraft it is building. Hence, short time space trip, e.g. flying to moon or leaving earth short suborbital flights, staying on space to viewing our earth , even long time space trip, e.g. flying to space station,spends more than one to two weeks. They may be future any one wealth space traveller's space trip leisure choice.

Some companies already conduct modest experiments on the space station, such as Merall Research laboratories, which has grown crystals of antibodies, and mode in space, which is testing the manufacture of higher quality optical communications fiber in the weightlessness of orbit. Hence, flying to moon and staying on space to viewing our earth space trips both ticket prices miust be more cheaper to compare long time spce trip, e.g. visiting space stations space trip. Axion space, a houston based company that arranges training and all aspects of the flights, is charging as much as US$55 million for a week long trip to the international space station. Blus Origin , Virgin Galactic had been planning attractive space trip. It focuses on views of earth space leisure activities when its space travelling customers can sit in its space rocket. Virgin Galactic was charging as much as US$250, 000 per seat on its spaceship. HOwever, these both space planes have a waiting list of about 600 passengers.

ON conclusion, in the future, the different kinds of space trips may include: short journey viewing earth, 15 to 30 minutes, visiting to moon, about one days , even it is possible that visiting space station, one to two weeks.

Even it is possible that any one space traveller can attempt to live one night in space hotel, if human can build hotels on moon, when human can confirm moon can build hotels , then flying to moon to live one night space trip experience may be implement in possible. I believe that any one space leisure provider can attract many space passengers to choose their viewing earth short time staying space trip, visiting moon, living space hotels, visiting space stations to live one night space leisure trip, So, any one space trip leisure provider can attempt to evaluaate whether implementing "living moon hotel" or " visiting space station" or viewing our earth any one space trip is possible in order to raise future any one potential space traveller individual leisure desire. However, the main considerable points, they need to evaluate whether they ought charge how much space trip ticket or seat price for every passenger. Also, they need build confidence to let every passenger feels their space rocket is safe to sit to leave our earth and come back our earth again absolutely. Hence, all of these are important factors to influence future any one space tourism leisure provider their success, if they expect to develop their space trips businesses in long time.

CHAPTER THREE

Space travel marketing strategy

Any space travel organization needs have good marketing strategy to prepare how to operate its space travelling leisure business in order to attract many space travelling clients to choose its space travelling service. I shall indicate these different strategies aspects whey they are needed to be concerned as below:

(1) On concept of spacecraft design aspect

Firstly, on concept aspect, any one space travelling leisure company needs have at least one spacecraft to catch clients to fly to space to travel. So how to design the spacecraft and its quality and safety and comfortable environment spacecraft machine concept aspect issue which is one challenge to be concerned. Because many space travelling passengers ususally concern whether the spacecraft is safe, comfortable , good quality, as well as the space travelling leisure providers also need to concern whether the spacecraft is less time and energy saving efficient use, less manufactory operating cost and durable.

In general, space travelling leisure provider expects the spacecraft or spacecraft vehicle can be uesed long time. The spacecraft will be expected to utilize previous flight rated and proven technologies to from the basis for manufacturing spacecraft vehicles , and will incorporate the latest modern avionics and flight system for answering safety, reliability and economical operation.

In general, the spacecraft will be designed to carry two crew and approximately, 10,000 pounds of cargo, depending on the ultimate weight of the spacecraft. Relying on flight hardware to maintain the space station, such as Moon or Mar space station is fpr any space travelling spacecrafts to reach these space travelling destinations to stay, it is also need to consider by many space travelling experts as risky, extremely, expensive cost sensitive for any space station travelling destination design arrangement in order to future every spacecraft can fly to any planets to stay on its space station safely.

● Outsourcing spacecraft concept design strategy

As a result, outsourcing strategy is one good method to help them to reduce cost in order to achieve to let every space travel passenger has safe space journey experience and capacity for safely launching a fully loaded (including crew and cargo). Outsourcing strategy is the launch role to a major contracor, they can concentrate on crew flight training, planning all passnegers and cargo capacoty, and preparing flight manifests, and will as a result, avoid the expense of maintaining a launch operation on a daily basis. In addition, by outsoucing the spacecraft manufacturing, the space travelling provider can avoid spending millions of dollars on facilities and equipment infrastructure and engineering manufacturing expertise.

(2) On deciding misson aspect

Secondly, on mission aspect, any space travelling journey needs have a clear mission to be planned how to achieve in order to ensure every space travelling passenger feel satisfactory in the space travelling journey. So, every whole space travelling journey arrangement, e.g. where will be the space travelling destination, how to check every space travelling planned passengers' bodies whether who are health to catch spacecraft to fly to space to travel or how to train every space travelling planned passenger to ensure whom can permit to catch spacecraft to fly to space to travel, how to arrange every space travelling journey entertainment and facilities to let either young or old age target passenger to enjoy the space trip to feel satisfactory, how to arrange different days of every space trip.

In the last few years, Virgin Galactic has been making new's headlines with its promises to provide space travel services, and announcement that it will soom offer, at quite a hefty price, trips to sub-orbit. It is generally agreed that sub-orbit exists 100 kilometres above the earth's sea-level (Von Der Dunk, 2012). Hence, Virgin Galactic will provide travel to where customers may experience weightlessness, as well as the sight of earth's curvature. Even more interesting is that Virgin Galactic is not the only company with such a mission,there are a few more that wish to offer the same type of service. For example, some companies even aim to provide an orbital type of flight.

Orbit flight suggests that humans would venture into outer space, where they might either orbit the earth or board the international space station (hereinafter: ISS). In addition, some envision space hotels, moon visitations and mining asteroids. Although at first such statement might seem for one must point out that a "space hotel" is already in earth's orbit and that diligent progress through flight tests is almost made the commercial aspect of regular space travel a reality; it is only the question of time and readiness for the companies to make their long-awaited and open a new industry of present day economics (Klemm & Markkanen, 2011; Berry , 2012).

So, every space travelling mission is to ensure that reliable, technologically-sophisicated competitively-priced flight certified spacecraft are designed and properly maintained when performing their every assigned space travelling journey mission. The space traveller leisure provider will need to provide a carefully selected array of techologies that are capable of meeting the requirements of travelling into earth orbit. It will emphasize affordability, reliability, safety, customer service and responsiveness in responding to customer's space travelling requirements.

For this space tourism leisure mission example, it many include these objectives , such as below:

One trip into space, sending a space vehicle of a certain make and with a specify capacity on a space mission, provides the various grades of a core service, such as a space mission including issues such as waiting and delivery times, personal attention and advice, amenities and facilities, ensure quality assurance, it is the planned and system activities implemented in a quality system. So that quality requirements for a product or service will be fulfilled. It aims at preventing high-risk adverse events, or reducing thei impact, provides excellent customer satisfaction, it is a measure of how products and services meet the space travelling customer expectations, customer satisfaction is also always evaluated in relationship of every space travelling ticket price of the space travelling entertainment service and spacecraft product comfortable environment feeling and good leisure arrangement for every space travelling leisure journey.

(3) On space tourism leisure organization managment aspect

Thirdly, on space tourism leisure organization management aspect, it is also important to influence efficient and excellent space service performance to be provided to satisfy every space travel organization management team needs to be consists of experienced professionals who have successfully management and operated companies specializing in the aerospace industry for a number of years.

Their knowledge and contacts within the space industry will prove invaluable in assisting the space tourism leisure provider in the achievement of its goals and objectives. In individuals on the team components that up a spacecraft tourism development organization, and have unique experience in the design, construction, operations and maintenance of the major functions will developing spacecraft for launching into orbit. Every spacecraft will be built and maintained utilizing the same high standards of quality, within budget and well within time constraints.

Hence, every space tourism provider needs have one excellent management leaders to manage every space tourism service staffs to serve passengers in order to achieve excellent service performance to let them every one to feel satisfactory, during their every space tourism journey (trip).

(4) On target audience prediction aspect

On target audience prediction aspect, every space trip needs have identifies target travelling passenger in order to concentrate to choose the most popular and satisfactory space travelling journey for their identified needs.

For primary audiences example, it can include space enthusiasts and educational families both. Space enthusiasts target are usually young people and they are only 20% over 65 age old people target space ethusiasts who will be the future potential space tourism target consumers as well as the educational families target who will aspect owning educational experience for children , who is the explicit reason to visit space, either he/she has interest in history of space exploration or he/she has interest in future of space exploration or he/she feels that spce trip looked like fun.

KSCVC Visots (2013) indicated that future top markets, ranked by high visitation against space enthusiasts and educational families space tourism passengers, the US cities will include: Orlando, NYC, Miami, Tampa Bay, Chicago, West plam, Philadelphia, Atlanta, Boston, Washington, DC and San Francisco cities. So, future US space travelling market will be the top one in the world.

(5) On space objective aspect

On space objective aspect, instead of any one space tourism leisure organization concerns how to achieve its mission to satisfy all space tourism passengers leisure needs. Although, it is the major missin for space tourism leisure industry. But they can not neglect what the objectives are in order to develop or achieve long term space tourism leisure missions more easily.

The objectives main open space key issues can include such as: Providing an adequate supply of land to meet the future needs of strategic opn space links, natural areas and recreational facilities on any future space tourism destinations, increasing pressure for public access to open space areas with conservation values, competing interests between adjoining land use and development on public open space and its user groups, use of public open space and recreational resources for drainage purposes, raising higher space traveller hotel residential development placing increased pressure on the demand for public open space planet land use aim and developing public open space mor intensive leisure and sport activities on any future new space tourism planet destinations.

When the space tourism leisure providers have long term objectives to attempt to solve above these any one of key issues. It will ahve a more clear objective to achieve its long term space tourism leisure business market. It's long term objectives can include such as below:

To identify existing and future active and passive recreation needs and social trends of future space tourism visitors; to provide a wide range of high quality and accessible public open space public land areas to encourage physical activity and social interaction to meet the existing and future needs of space travelling visitors; to identify existing gaps in the public open space network and develop any different kinds of space trip arrangement to satisfy the different identified target space traveller individual needs; to protect enhance and increase landcrapt values of public open space land use; to recognize the hierarchy of public open space assets; equitably distributing open space resources; access to facilities and a diverse range of opportunities to incorporate the drainage function in public open space travelling destination areas without detriment to safely, environmental, visual and recreational values.

So, these development of any space planets howo to use their lands objectives will bring long term space travelling destination beneficial advantages to raise to build the space hotels, space swimming pools, space gardens, space cinemas, space sport places to let future space travelers can stay in Mars or Moon planet destinations to enjoy these leisure facilities and they can feel which are similar to our earth leisure facilities attractively. These space buildings are important to attract future space travellers to catch spacecraft to fly to Mars or Moon planet to travel in possible because it is fun and exciting space trip when these leisure facilities can be built on Moon or Mars to let space travellers to stay short days in either these two planets to live their space hotels. So how to build any one of these space leisure building which is another important objective for any future space tourism leisure business, instead of how to arrange any space destination trip objective. So, any space tourism leisure provider ought not neglect how to achieve these two main space tourism objectives.

However, these are key questions continually asked regarding the viability of space tourism. They concern financial, marketing and political communities. Their concerns can be best addredded in a properly, comprehensive business plan. Some questions can not be answered definitively at this time. Hoever, knowledge of the concerns and developing space businesses in any space traveling leisure planning stages and efforts to raise capital in the following questions, every spce tourism leisure business leader needs to concern this questions as below:

Can the space tourism industry into a profitable enonomic industry?

Are challenges related to financing, marketing, business methodologies or a combination of all of these facets?

Can the proponents of space tourism to be proven business tools and methodologies in their presentation of an acceptable business plan?

Can at least a cost effective, certified passenger space tourism journey to be developed for space tourism?

What effects will influence space-tourism businesses of NASA begins selling seats on the US space shuttle to civilian space tourists?

All above questions will be every new space tourism leisure businessman who needs to concern questions in order to achieve whose marketing strategy more successfully. Consequently, marketing strategy is important to be prepared in order to follow corrective steps to achieve every space tourism leisure business missions and objectives more easily.

● Space tourism leisure behavioral economic
consumption model

In space tourism leisure industry, due to every time space trip needs the space travelling planner to plan how much budget to consume expensive spce ticket price. So, it seems that the target customers will be rich or high income level young people or the retirement rich old people target customer group.

So, it brings this question: How to persuade these rich or high income young people or rich retirement old people to prefer to spend spce tourism leisure at least one time in their life?

It is one valuabe research question to every future space tourism leisure provider. I shall indicate the successful factors to analyze how to persuade them to accept this kind of potential space travelling leisure in behavioral economic personal consumption view point, in order to explain the cause and effect relationship between of these factors as below:

(1) Economic environment variable factor

Firstly, it is economic environment variable factor whether it can influence to space tourism leisure consumption changing. As I discuss about economic environment variable issue will influence consumption behavior changing. For space tourism leisure case, it is not now kind of essential consumption leisure product to every one. So , even the rich or high income people who will be influences to seek this kind of leisure to play, it the economic environment is improved, it will influence they have positive attitude and interest to choose this kind of leisure consumption. However, if the economic environment is worse, it will influence they have negative attitude and no interest to choose this kind of leisure consumption, due to space travel is one kind of expensive leisure consumption to every one.

Hence, in this space tourism leisure industry, it does not ensure that the rich or high income people must be persuade to choose this kind of expensive space tourism entertainment in whose holiday or retirement time. They can have the common tourism entertainment to go to different countries to travel many times in our earth. Otherwise, space tourism leisure is more expensive to compare common earth tourism leisure , it means that the rich or high income people only spend one time spacecraft catching to fly to space to travel in their life, it is more difficult to every space traveler like to catch spacecraft to fly to space to travel more than one time, due to he/she had attempted to catch spacecraft to fly to space to travel to own space travel experience, he/she will feel enough satisfactory and enjoyment in common. Hence, it is possible that future many rich or high income people only like to spend one time space tourism leisure, then they won't continue to spend this kind of tourism entertainment again in their life.

Thus, space tourism leisure providers need to arrange any special or attractive space tourism leisure to persuade these high income or rich target clients to consume, when the economic environment will change worse. The Europen space agency (ESA), defines this phenomenon between economic environment variable and space tourism client growth or falling number relationship as: " space tourism is an execution of sub-orbital flight by privately finded and/or privately operated vehicles and the technology development driven by space tourism market."

it seems that space vehicle is one attractive travelling desire tool will be one attractive selling point to influence space tourism leisure consumer individual entertainment choice or attitude to be changed to positive leisure consumption attitude to prefer to play this kind of space tourism activities when economic environment changes to worse. Hence, when economic environment is worse, the economic wore changing factor will influence the space travelling planner individual leisure consumption desire, even it will influence the rich or high income young people or rich retirement people target customer both groups.

As (ESA, 2008) indicated space vehicle will be one kind of attractive leisure tool for spce traveler. So, I suggest that space tourism lesiure journey arrangement needs to include that such as : the space travelers can catch space vehicle to move on Moon or Mars plants land to feel what the different feeling is between during they are catching public transportation tool, such as bus or taxi during the are catching these transportation tools on earth land and during they are catching space vehicle tools on Mars or Moon planet's lands. It is so exicting and fun catching space vehicle tool experience on these both Mars or Moon planets' lands to the young and old age space travelling passengers. Because every space vehicle's speed is not very fast and it will move on Moon or Mars planets slowly. So, any aged pace travelling passengers can attempt to play this kind of space facilities leisure after they catched spacecraft to fly to these both Mars or Moon planet to stay. They can spend half hour or one hour, even more than one hour to catch the space vehicle to go to anywhere on Mars or Moon to travel. It is possible that they can find exciting and undiscovered things on these both planets.

So, catching space vehicle to go to anywhere on either these both planets journey, it will one essential part of space travelling journey during the economic environment is changed to worse. It is extra attractive space travelling leisure journey to attract space tourism consumer individual leisure desire when economic environment is worse.

Hence, from this perspective then space tourism could be understood as a section of the tourism industry mainly based on technological development, progression and its activitity being related specifically to sub orbital flights. So, if future space tourism providers expect whether the global economic environment changing will be better or worse which won't influence space tourism leisure consumption desire to be changed. The space tourism leisure providers need to persuade the space tourism planners feel space tourism would have to be treated like an already exciting part of the tourism industry. It means that space tourism leisure is one kind of tourism leisure choice to replace common earth tourism leisure consumption. When travelers feel space tourism is another tourism leisure to replace which can replace common earth tourism leisure. It will avoid the worse economic environment changing factor to reduce the rich or high income young people or rich retirement old people whose space travelling leisure consumption desire.

Consequently , the question in relation to, in what kinds of space tourism journey message do space travel providers promote behind whether space vehicle journey promotion message which is needed when economic environment will change worse. I shall be asked, as understanding the meaning in which space tourism is being marketed, communicated is seen as a factor , which can either positively contribute to future development of the tourism industry or lead into prolonging or seen stopping the space tourism industry from its progression.

(2) Space tourism leisure journey management factor

Secondly, space tourism leisure jounrey management factor, how to arrange every space tourism leisure journey which will be one important factor to influence space tourism planner individual tourism consumption desire.

In general, it can includes these several forms of space tourism leisure activities in every space lesiure trip arrangement. The following classification of space tourism include: Terrestria spce tourism (i.e. NASA visit centre, space movies, online space experience); Atmospheric space tourism (i.e. : MIG 31 flight, zero G. flights) and astro (orbita) tourism (i.e.: trips to the international space station-beyond earth orbit) (Cater 2010, Crouch et al. 2009).

Instead of US domestic space tourism market is potential, next country is Japan. First, the study is made by Collins et. al (1994, 1996) in Japan on 3030 research participants, showed that 80% of respondents under the age of 50 were willing to travel to space and out of them 20% were willing to pay year's salary for the space travel experience. Yet, it could be citicized that the Japan people age group of under 50 could be too broad, in general different generations under one groups. nest besides the willingness to go to space, the Japanese study showed respondents motivations for travelling to space, including any fun and exciting attractive space tourism journey, e.g. interest in space walk, catching space vehicle or driving space vehicle on the either Moon or Mars planets, earth view, zeo gravity experience, livin gin space hotels one night or more, watching movies in space cinemas, swimming in space pools, visiting space gardens, running in space sport centers, catching spacecrafts to view earth or Moon or Mars planets.

Hence, it seems attractive space tourism journey can persuade another country's space travelling planners, such as Japanese attempts to satisfy whose space tourism needs. So, different kinds of attractive space trip journey arrangement will be one important factor to influence young and old age travelling consumption desire. It implies that attractive space tourism journey will be one influential factor to encourage other countries tourism consumers attempt to another kind of leaving earth tourism leisure. So, any space tourism trip destinations and leisure facilities arrangement must need to satisfy space traveler individual leisure needs and every space trip must be more fun, exciting and comfortable and enjoyable feeling to compare general tourism journey in earth. Due to general earth tourism leisure will be space tourism leisure's competitive or replaced leisure product and service. Hence, space trip destinations and leisure facilities choice will be one important factor to influence space travelling planner's consumption desire.

Every space travelling planner will compare general earth travelling leisure's destinations and leisure facilities arrangement whether the space travelling trip arrangement , leisure facilities arrangement and food arrangement, space vehicle or spacecraf leisure comfortable influence issues which will have more satisfactory enjoyable feeling to compare general earth tourism leisure and their spending expenditure to every space trip whether is value or is not value.

Consequently, economic environment changing factor and space trip and leisure facilities arrangement factor which both will influence any space tourism planner individual consumption desire mainly. So, space tourism businessmen ought concern these two aspects of factors how and when will change to adapt any country's potential space traveler's space tourism changing taste and needs in order to follow the new space tourism changing needs easily.

Space tourism market moral ethic risk threats

What are space tourism moral ethic risk during the space businessmen operate this businesses as well as what market threats who will encounter to face difficulties ? I shall give actul cases to explain how and why these challenges will cause to influence any new space tourism businesses development successfully.

(1) Potential accidents aspect

Firstly, space travelers will concern that public reactions to potential accidents aspect during they are catching spacecrafts to travel to space. In fact, it is moral ethic responsibility to any space tourism leisure providers to provide safe, comfortable and non accident occurrence in their whole space trip. Because once time accident will cause any one of space passenger hurt or death. So , it must be any space tourism businessmen responsibilities to concern whether they have enough confidence to ensure none any accident occurrences in every space tourism trip.

Hence, in space tourism industry, government needs have public policy to threaten or prohibit any space tourism leisure providers neglect to often check and ensure any spacecraft machines or equipments are regular opeations, as well as often renew new spacecraft machines when they are old to be used. The policy is a force effort to need them to abide every space tourism leisure safe responsibility to ensure or guarantee any one of spacecraft won't have accident occurrences during it has left earth to fly to space in whole space trip journey from the beginning to the end till to the spacecraft come to earth safely.

Hence, this policy forces any space tourism leisure providers concern to put a monetary value on increased or reduced risk of death, the " value of statistical live", used to characterize when the benefit of safety regulation is worth the cost such regulation improves. So, the country government and the country's space tourism leisure providers both have responsibilities to guarantee all space tourism passengers' life safety. It must not allow any death or hurt occurrences during every space tourism trip.

Even, the country government can have legal action to publish any space tourism leisure providers, when their every space tourism trip has occurred accidents, e.g. fire accident occurrence in spacecarft or spacecrat machines are broken to be damaged and need to be repaired during the space tourism trip. It will threaten to reduce trip accident occurrence, such as this cases.

The commercial space ventures may present risk to property as well, such as a fire starting on the ground by launch-related material or problems presented by space debris.

In principle, liability law can provide incentive to deter carelessness that could lead to the destruction of property, although statutory (rather than common law) assignments of liability for commercial launches are somewhat problematic.

Consequently, if the space tourism leisure provider expected to grow space tourism passenger number in long -term time, it must need to ensure none any accidents can occur during any space trip. Otherwise, the space tourism passengers can choose another space tourism leisure provider to replace its spce tourism leisure easily.

(2) Space tourism destinations and space tourism entertainment facilities safe arrangement challenges aspect

Secondly, it is space tourism destinations and space tourism entertainment facilities safe arrangement challenges. Nowadays, commercial space travel is looking more like a real possibility than science fiction. The usual ethical issues related to the safety of the space destination choices and the space tourism entertainment facilities, e.g. space vehicles, space hotels, space swimming pools, space sport centers, space cinemas, space gardens, space farming lands. In this strange space environment and safety concerns are just the beginning as there are othe interesting questions, such as below:

What likely would be a fair process for commercializing or claiming property in any space planets? Such as Moon or mars, when any future space tourism leisure providers who need to build above these any one of space entertainment facilities on these planets to provide to their space travelling customers to play.

How to distribute and manage these any lands ownership to these future space tourism providers fairly and legally?

How likely would a separatist movement be among space settlements to want to be free and independent states?

How to ensure above future space entertainment facilities and space entertainment places are in the safe space environment to be provided to any space travelers to play in any planets, e.g. Moon or Mars etc. planets.

So, concerning how to arrange space entertainment facilities to provide to space tourism clients to play in any safe space environment issue, it will be another concerning question to every space tourism leisure providers. When they decide to choose anywhere to the space hotels, space swimming pools, space gardens, space cinemas or space farming lands or space sport centers. These space buildings will need to be built in the safe, on stable stone lands environment and none any natural distaster, such as large wind or space underground water etc. unpredictable space natural distasterr attack to these space buildings suddenly. Because it has responsibility to any space tourism leisure providers to guarantee any one of these space buildings are safe to be built in the planet's safe land environment. It aims to achieve none any accident occurrences during their space tourism clients are staying to enter these any one of space buildings to visit or play any space entertainment facilities safely, e.g. space vehicle.

So, they must need to ceck anywhere the space planet's places to be ensured safe to build any buildings. Then, they can choose the suitable locations to build space entertainment facilities or buildings more confidently.

In fact, any space entertainment facilities, e.g. space hotels, space farming lands as well as space transportation tools, e.g. spce vehicle, spacecraft , these things will be value to be concerned to any space tourism leisure providers and it is business moral ethic responsibility to every one of them, when they plan to develop their space tourism business in any planets.

(3) Space tourism market competition challenge aspect

Thirdly, any provate space tourism development leisure businesses will face market competitive challenge, such as large spacefaring countries, e.g. US, UK have possible to dominate future space tourism leisure business (government can own space tourism leisure business). They will be main actors in space were nation-states. Large spacefaring counties can build the space vehicles, that can take people and cargo into orbit and to the Moon, or Mars crafted international space law and shaped the main investments in space tourism leisure technology.

So, it is possible that the own space technological developed countries, such as US, UK, these countries governemts will have possible to operate public fund to support space tourism leisure business. It implies that private space tourism leisure businesses will face public space tourism leisure business and themselve private space tourism leisure business market competition in space tourism leisure industry.

If these two countries governments also participate this private space tourism leisure market. It will raise market threats to any private space tourism organizations.

Whether will developed countries governments participate private space tourism market? It is possible that new commercial actors began to enter the space tourism leisure industry, looking to disrupt both space launch services ans use space in new exotic ways. For example, the US government also moved its purposeful degradatoin of the global positioning system (GPS), so US government will have effort to dominate GPS global positioning system communication business also. As this GPS communication business case, future US government has possible to decide to participate space tourism leisure business also.

However, in the future, space tourism leisure industry may contribute even more the developed countries, e.g. American, England economy. Space tourism and resource recovery, e.g. mining on planet, Moons and asteroids in particular may become large parts of that space tourism industry if these countries governments participated to this space tourism industry development. Of course, their viability rests on a range of factors, including costs , future regulation, international market competivitive problems and assumption about space technological development. However, these is increasing optimism in these areas of economic production to bring human space tourism leisure enjoyment and space mining resource development benefits. But the space economy is not just about what happens in orbits or how that alters life on the ground. The growth of this economy can also contribite to new innovations across all future possible unpredictable or undiscovered technological development, instead of space tourism leisure or space mining resource exploitation development.

Consequently, any space development technological governments will have possible to bring economic benefits from either only private space tourism leisure organizations or governments and private space tourism leisure both organizations cooperate to participate to achieve space tourism misson to contribute to global economic development and create new jobs to be employed in space labor supply market.

● Can space tourism business bring
economy benefits

It is fact that space tourism activities have a positive and beneficial impact on eveyday life and society and this help space travelers to understand that, despite the high space ticket prices of any space tourism leisure choices. However, space tourism will bring scientific knowledge and technological knowhow and jobs to bring humn tangible or untangible both benefits. I shall indicate these benefits as below:

Although, space tourism leisure seems only leisure activities to be consumed to satisfy any space tourism individual travelling need. However, it can assign space scientists to research and attempt discovery these intangible benefits: Such as tele-communications revolution, satellite weather forecasting, mapping mineral exploration, water resource management diaster mitigation, national security or other undiscovered untangible benefits. Because every spacecraft needs to plan to fly to space, and it will reach any space planet stations, e.g. Mars, Moon planet when it visits these any one planet, the space scientists can attempt to find new undiscovered space resource , e.g. mining or finding new undiscovered satellite weather forecasting method when they can reach these planets to attempt to do space scientifical investigtion to research new space resource , or find any space stones attack to our methods to avoid earth disaster occurrence (national security mission), instead of the spacecraft catchs space passengers to visit these planets to enjoy these planets space entertainment facilities in their space trip journeys.

(1) On space resource benefit aspect

Hence, the space tourism intangible benefits include: space exploration and international cooperation is developing sophisticted space technologies by nations. For example, the images of distant stars and glaxies using Hubble telescope, research laboratory such as international space station to conduct experiments in biology, human biology, physics, Astronomy and meteorology under microgravity environment and testing of the spacecraft systems will be required for space tourism missions to the Moon and Mars. In the future, human would be able to have unlimited and clean solar energy from space for our industries as well as heating and lighting our homes. In the near future , it would be possible to disposed-off our nuclear waste safely and unexpensively and released towards the sun using a space elevator. We many become a space tourist in earth orbit or on the Moon or Mars. We may carry and extra-terrestial mining and even introduce the development of a multi-planet economy.

(2) On education benefit aspect

Another on education benefit aspect, space tourism can let space travelers to feel actual space learning experiences, during the spacecraft is flying in the space. Their space environment learning experience can include, for example: How many spacecraft have been launched by a given country? How many phone calls are made over a satellite? How many lives could be saved by resue satellites? How they feel differences when they are living in one space hotels, they are swimming in the swimming pools, they are visiting the space garden, they are running in one space sport centers, they are visiting in one space farming land, they are sitting or driving one space vehicle on planet land, or they are catching one spacecraft.

These space learning experience will let they feel what the actual differences between space environment and earth environment. It is one humankind learning experience education service in any space planet's Moon or Mars remote areas, bringing information and tourism entertainment facilities to the masses. The space experience learning knowledge can provide data to let these space travelers to know, such as how ships can be safe at sea, monitoring the threat of pollution, how enhancing durable medical instruments for better health-care enabling hikers and skiers to be located when lost, many more. So, it seems space tourism can bring much positive benefits as no negative impact on space activitied has been found by the society , the investments are made by the nations on space activites are justified and not the waste of money.

● What are the tangible social and economic benefits brought from space tourism?

In most advanced economies space tourism or space resource exploitation industry is seen as an enabler that improves lives and helps to develop both economic and social spheres. Space industry economic can include these aspect: Application of space technology to space tourism navigation, meteorological forcasting and broadcast of on live television and internet connectivity to lesser-known applications, such as precision agriculture, transport, tracking, resource extraction and monitoring of utility networks.

Additional application exists in the disaster monitoring and relif, insurance and military applications. Thus, data coming from satellites is important to all economic sectors, making the world a better and safer place.

International space tourism experience would suggest that space travelling leisure businesses deliver value by providing a central point for academia industry , defence and foreign entities to collaborate among themselves and with government and to facilitate the flow of knowledge and capital.

How can space tourism industry maximize the socio-economic benefits? In fact, our growing use of space derived data and systems is our growing dependence on a better and safer sapce planet, e.g. Moon or Mars and to provide space tourism safe services that space travelling service that space traveler all benefit from industry in telecommunication , health, transport , banking , security and climate change monitoring.

The space tourism positive influence result is long term, the positive contribution to our quality of life is real. In other word, the world for space tourism leisure activities is changing the internationally space tourism sector is experiencing a profound revolution.

In conclusion, space tourism leisure countries with historical leadership in space tourism have been under positive as a result of a tough financial environment leading to the definition of their space travelling technology priorities. In the meantime, new space entertainment travelling leaders, such as US, UK , even China, India have ambitions in space tourism through massive investments in the development of their capabilities in space travelling leisure business aspect.

So, the future space travelling entertainment market is large, due to China and India both have many rich people and high income people, who expect to consume in space tourism leisure trip at least one time in their lifes. Consequently, worldwide space tourism entertainment industry players are rethinking their busines models and strategies as they experience discuptive innovations, competitive space tourism entertainment and new drivers impacting the spacecraft and any space entertainment facilities manufacturing on Moon or Mars planet, launch and space tourism entertainment related businesses. Thus, we can in fact in talk about a new space tourism business, in which more and more innovative applications of space tourism data are developed dependence on space tourism data in everyday life rises and increasing share of economic growth relies on the space tourism market both in terms of opportunity benefits , e.g. India and China spce tourism potential market development and any concern space tourism job creation to every countries. Hence, space tourism development can bring positive economic benefits to any countries.

Chapter 4
Space flight safe factor

To operate one space flight exploration organization, it needs to concern human safe flight factor. I shall indicate it needs to have these three stages to further develop its space exploration to continue to improve its safe space flight for every time of space flight.

Human future space flight missions will include these three stages to continue journey into space. The first stage is short term, NASA's return to flight after the Columbia accident. The second stage is mid term. What is needed to continue flying the shuttle fleet until a replacement means for human access to space and for other shuttle capabilities is available, and the third stage is long term, future directions for the kinds in space. Therefore, the space exploration organization can arrange the three stages to carry out any future space exploration activities. I believe it can improve every time of space flight more safe because it can ensure its space rocket engineering can be improved to raise safe level to let space people to catch to leave our Earth.

However, any human future space flight, which must be enhanced safety of flight when carry on any experimenting space flight exploration missions. Because NASA's safety performance is a very important factor to influence any space people confidence to catch every sky rocket to leave our Earth to do any space exploration activities. So, eliminating and catching rocket risks will be any beginning and end than during the middle of any space flight exploration journeys.

Space people's life is the most important assets of any space exploration journeys. Because of the dangers of ascent and re-entry, because of unknown space environment and because we are still relative new comers, operation of shuttle and indeed all human space flight must be viewed as a development activity.

Thus, any every time space flight exploration missions will need to encourage to invent new space transportation engines (machine) or fuel, e.g. nuclear fuel to reduce the any space exploration journey accident risks and achieves to spend the fastest time to arrive any new space exploration destination. Thus, I believe any new space exploration flight will improve the space transportation technology and invent more new fuel and new space rocket manufacturing materials for future human any unknown space exploration flight demand. The three stages of improving space transportation include as below:

The beginning stage, for example, the space shuttle is as somehow comparable to civil or military air transport. They are not comparable; the inherent risks of spaceflight are serious higher. The recognition of human spaceflight as a developmental activity requires a shift in focus from operations and meeting schedules to a concern for the risks involves. Thus, the space transportation tools will be improved to protect space passengers safety: the improving the ability to tolerate it, repairing the damage on a timely basis, reducing unforeseen events from the loss of crew and vehicle, exploring all options for survival, such as provisions for crew escape systems and safe havens , barring unwarranted departures from design standards and adjusting standards only under the most safety-driven process.

The mid-term stage, the present shuttle is not very safe to fly in space. Thus, focus on safe return to flight is very important to every space flight journey rules , they leave Earth and arrive any another new planet destination, then come back our Earth again in every space exploration journey (flight). Thus, the energy will be space transportation tool one important factor. If the space transportation tool has enough supply, which won't stay in space and can not fly in space suddenly. Thus, the every time of the human space flight will be taken more time and effort then would be reasonable to expect prior to return to flight. Thus, human space exploration organization needs have higher reliability organization structure to manage every space flight, e.g. one is separating technical authority from the function of managing schedules and cost. Another is an independent safety and mission assurance organization.

It is the capability for effective systems integration perhaps even more challenging than these organizational changes are the cultural changes requires. Thus, the cultural to safe and effective space rocket operations are real and substantial. If the space exploration organization has good culture to let every staffs can communicate easily. I believe the every time space exploration accident will be reduced. Examples include: the tendency to keep knowledge of problems contained within a center or program, technical decisions, without in -depth, peer-reviewed technical analysis, and an unofficial hierarchy or system created by placing excessive power in one office. Such factors interfere with open communication, the shared of lesson learned, cause duplication and expenditure of resources and create a burden for managers to reduce undesirable characteristics threaten safety.

Thus, any space exploration trip, rocket equipment safety and check are very important factor to prepare for every time space flight. The reason is that space flight must guarantee any space people who can come back Earth, if the rocket equipment are poor and lack maintenance. The, the space people whose life is dangerous. Due any space exploration organization mission require human presence in space. For example, president John Kennedy's 1961 charge to send Americans to the moon and return then safely to Earth. Thus, the space exploration organization has attempted to carry out a similar high priority mission that would justify the expenditure of resources on a scale equivalent to those allocated for project Apollo. Also, the space exploration organization has had to participate in the give and take of the normal political process in order to obtain the resources needed to carry out its programs.

Another main successful factor in the final stage, the space exploration organization needs have a clearly defined long term space mission to commit over the past decade to improve future space exploration flight safety by developing a second generation space transportation system. So, for long term, the space exploration organization should need to plan for future space transportation capabilities without making them dependent on technological breakthroughs.

For example, mission for a post Apollo effort that involved full development of low-Earth orbit, permanent outposts on the moon, and initial journeys to Mars planet. Since that rejection, these objective, have reappeared as central elements in many proposals, setting a long term vision for any space exploration flight programs in the future.

Thus, space organization future space exploration mission for 21 St century is to lead the exploration and development of the space frontier, advance science, technology and enterprise and building institutions and systems that make accessible vast new resources and support human settlements beyond Earth orbit from the highland of the Moon to the plains of Mars. Thus, the space exploration organization limit is to conduct the research required to plan missions to Mars and/or other distant destinations. This is the most safe space flight distance limit by the space rocket equipment, machine installation , quality and effort to guarantee space people life safety when who catch the space rocket life safety when who catch the rocket to leave Earth to arrive any space destination in any space flight. However, human travel to destinations beyond Earth orbit has not been adopted because it is too far space flight to cause accident risk. Hence, space exploration organization future invention of long term need is that the role of new space transportation capabilities in enabling whatever space goals need to choose to pursue for human present in Earth orbit vision.

In conclusion, space exploration organization needs to in-depth examination space shuttle safe issue, how to reach an inescapable design of the space shuttle, because that the design was based in many aspects on how absolute technologies and because the space shutter is now an aging system , but still developmental in character, it is in the space organization is interest to replace the shuttle as soon as possible as the primary aim for transporting humans to and from Earth orbit.

- ● Space exploration organization mission and strategy

Space exploration organization communication strategy

I recommend any space exploration organization needs to the message concerns how the role of humans are actual physical presence in space exploration missions succeed. Because the positive message will give good idea of space exploration and then design and build means to carry out right space exploration direction to let humans to know whether any space exploration missions' goals, objectives and what humans benefits (welfares) who can earn.

The message includes such as these primary role of humans, therefore, is to provide the inspiration and create the vision which produces the motivation in those who then go on to make it a reality, e.g. the space exploration mission is to bring their human intellectual capability to bear in designing the technical systems required for space transportation and devising the scientific experiments associated with space exploration from its beginnings.

Thus, any space exploration organization needs to let humans to know whether what benefits humans will earn after it carries out any space exploration experiments possibly. I believe that the exploration of the Earth's great expanse (the sea, the undersea world, air and land) is the ultimate role played by humans in body and in mind, and apply their intelligence, emotions and most importantly of all, their superior cognitive performance. So, this is the role now played by astronauts, explorers in the true sense of the world.

Why does space exploration organization need to be the role of communicator? The reason is because there is the role that space organization's need to play as communicators, journalists or other communication professional. It is they who provide the link between those involved in the project and taxpayer, who are entitled to be informed about the fascinating news on space.

Moreover, space exploration organization staffs need to give message to let humans to know why these playing roles are entirely human specific and can not be fulfilled by machines. For example, roles prior to human intervention, such as accompanying humans and performing tasks, which are repetitive and unpleasant out satellites too high a risk. By sending out satellites to explore our solar system humans have already begun to explore universe into reality Robots. On the other hand, may be things, but they are not visionaries and nor are they inventors or explorers. Any achievement they accomplish are in fact space organization staffs who designed and programmed them. Also, humans remain the best available cognitive machine in any environment that may be subject to significant variations relative to the model initially made of it. Thus, space exploration organization needs to explain, such as why in the general context of space exploration, even of most missions are robotic, remains technology challenges, it presents push engineers to the very limits of what can be achieved.

In the future, humans will earn these benefits or from any space explorations new invention possibly, such as fuel cells, the microcomputer, high performance materials, medical advances, new management techniques for major projects, quality and reliability control in industry etc. The most important space exploration organization needs to positive message to let these groups of people to human what which is doing in our societies. Then, which will cause different actors to become involved from thinkers, visionaries and inspirational figures in the form of writers and film makers to scientists, engineers, philosophers, politicians, economists, physicians, journalists, authors, space travelers (astronauts), but also adults and children space story book readers alike. Thus, space exploration organization is truly multi disciplinary enterprise. Moreover, in the present day, normal escapes being concerned by space, as much due to its contribution to daily life and the knowledge it beings of the Solar system and the universe. It seems space exploration organization will influence human past history will be changed to develop. Whether it brings positive or negative change. The space organization must have responsibility to keep its any space exploration missions leader position in our Earth. It implies it is also one social responsible organization for future global human benefit (welfare).

Also space exploration organization needs to let humans know what it's future aims (intentions) are to let humans know whether why it plan to implement. Such as it needs to choose destination has typically been the Moon, it had increasingly come to focus its attention on Mars and even further afraid. Moreover, it also needs to know humans to know the modes of future space transportation which described have tended to be those of the period concerned: ships, horses, birds, balloons, canons, rockets and even others of a more esoteric nature, even solar sail or nuclear soil further space transportation technology development. In addition, space exploration organization can need to describe where are further orbital space stations in space different locations and explained the various applications of satellites and spacecrafts to let human to know clearly.

Even, space exploration organization also need to let humans to know what are their technical challenges, it will encounter in any space exploration stages to let humans to know. Although, the complexity and changer involved in spaceflight is such for a long time to come there will be a need for experts, whose focus by necessity. So, the general public will know or recognize why it's technical challenges will cause and how it will attempt to solve these technical challenges. It aims to let humans to ensure more than 40 years of spaceflight, the adventive of space, which for technical reasons is inevitably reserved to a " happy few", remains very much the preserve of specialists, cooperation to research how to solve any technical challenges to achieve success in any space exploration mission consequently.

● Space exploration organization team leaders and their teams

The first team members are program chiefs and mission message are request to the be backroom generals with a great many human qualities. They must having to achieve great technical exploits and manage their teams with care when at the same time ensuring they deliver in timing and one budget. Even the very best robot-machines and computers available are of no help to them in coming up with the initial idea and architecture for their systems. Indeed, in that initial stages, some program chiefs, even insist on their management team using only paper and pencil writing. Once the concept has been defined, they then need computers to speed up and develop the project.

When these leader figures are fortunate enough to see their program in orbit and crowned with success, their experience and methods can be of use, to equally computer technical sectors. They can also be passed on to following generations, thus safeguarding, for reasons of economics and security, the know how acquired by their teams. Another team members are scientists and those responsible for the technical side of program are not generally skilled communicators by nature, those with communication to public , such " communicators" could be awarded special prizes. Communication on the space sector can't be left to " communication specialists". Otherwise, there is a risk, it will be perceived to be doomed to failure.

Space exploration organization education is such as strategy space exploration organization communicator, are there to inform, the teaching profession for its part, must perform a vital education role, helping people understand the universe in which they live. Space exploration represents a unique opportunity to explain the situation of our planet within the solar system, asking questions such as: How does the sun function? What are the origins of the Moon? Why does Venus have such a pronounced greenhouse effect? Is there or has there ever been life on Mars? Do asteroids pose a serious threat? There are all questions which today, our schools don't even attempt to answer. Thus, space exploration organization can be one educator role, instead of space explorer role.

Thus, space exploration organization has mission to assist universities to promote space exploration education knowledges. It brings this question: What other technological and scientific program is better equipped to meet these objective than space exploration , with its crewed emissions component. So crucial to the promotion of a European industry, so visible to the general public and so efficient in inducing younger generations to take up scientific and technical careers? Thus, the space education courses can include space exploration industrial applications, a new area of investigation to scientific fields, fundamental physics, cellular and vegetal biomedical research and human and animal physiological research etc. subjects. For example, teaching how to go to Mars or other planets and manage to live these will require a knowledge of how to energy in innovative ways for the purposes of managing electricity generation requirement will be to learn how to manage scare resources in an efficient way (air, water and waste recycling). So, teaching of progress will have to be made in advanced robotics in particular in the area of effective and human robot interaction.

In conclusion, all these space exploration science education knowledge will be important to be taught to let younger to pursue space resource exploration dream for human future live

- ● Space exploration organization's

Human space life science factor

What is human space life science strategy?

One space exploration organization needs have good human resource strategy to implement every space exploration mission. Critical to this expansion of human presence in space science will enable mission success by focusing on risk reduction and optimizing astronaut health an productivity through space organization's human-centered science, operations and engineering core capabilities.

Thus, the space life science strategy's strategical goals, and objectives were developed on the basis of a situational analysis conducted by key members of the space life science civil service and contractor

community, and are consistent with agency goals and scenarios for the future.

This strategy mission is to optimize human health and productivity for space exploration and its vision is to become the recognized world leader in human health, performance and productivity for space exploration . It's strategic goal are aimed at driving innovations in health and human system integration, adapting its portfolio and strategies to the changing environment and creating enthusiasm for space exploration through education. Also, the space life sciences human strategy aims to achieve every space exploration research more success, more efficient, focuses on client (human) needs and facilities communication of risk to public and the value of space life sciences to its stakeholders (governments, universities, societies).

How can human space life science strategy implement?

The space exploration organization needs to be dependent upon healthy, productive astronauts to achieve mission success. Thus, space people health are very important factor to influence their every time space flight in success. If the space people have unhealthy bodies , which will influence whose work performance and every time space exploration mission can't finish easily. Thus, the human space life science strategy needs to ensure every space person has health body to work efficiently and reduce whose death or accident risk when they are working in space environment, due to space environment is one strange bad color environment and it is very difference to our Earth environment to unsafe to work by these factors:

such as, it's temperature is low, cold and no air or oxygen to be supplied to let human to breathe and it has unknown diseases in space. Thus, they will face any life danger when are working in space environment. If space organization lacks one human space life science strategy to help them to fight any unknown attack from space environment. The, they are very dangerous to attempt to catch space rockets to leave our Earth to do any space exploration activities.

However, the space life science strategy can divide these three timeframes consistent with

- Near –term (1-5 years)
- Mid-term (6-10 years)
- Long-term (11-20 years)

The space life science strategy mission is that optimize human health and productivity for space exploration . Thus, all space life sciences human health and countermeasures research, medical operations, habitability and environmental factors activities, and directorate support functions are ultimately aimed at achieving this mission. Their activities enable mission success, optimizing human health and productivity in space before, during and after the actual space flight experience of their flight crews, and include support for ground-based functions.

The space life science strategy vision is to become the recognized world leader in human health, performance and productivity for space exploration. Thus, to achieve the vision for space exploration , they must drive human health, performance and productivity innovations, adapting

their strategy to the changing environment. To do this, the space exploration organization needs have a future scenario for space life science strategy such as below:

- Future core capabilities will include the expertise to address space medicine, the physiological and behavioral effects of space flight, space environment definition and space human factors.
- Research plans are on the basis of a standard –based risk mitigation approach to ensure goals are achieved.
- Civil servants will balance delivery of health and performance services and focused research and technology development with smart buyer and management expertise to integrate space life sciences efforts.
- Strategy relationships will be utilized to achieve the full complement of space life sciences core

capabilities necessary to achieve vision and enable mission success.

- Space life science strategy will transition from being a managing partner to a contributing partner, arranging the resources and innovations of other organizations to meet specific exploration needs, e.g. universities, government or business biomedicine organizations.
- Operations will effectively transition the space people skills and facilities from shuttle and assess and engage in additional government and

commercial space flight operations opportunities where appropriate.

● An expanded client base that may include additional international and academic partners , as well as commercial alliances.

Situation analysis

A situation analysis was conducted to determine its mission and to identify the factors most likely to influence its strategy development and affect achievement of its goals and objectives . It will trend to concern life sciences and space flight of internal and external environments. It needs to image these assumptions to decide its situation analysis as below:

Thus, the first assumption is that it needs to assume that human will continue to be an important component of the vision for space exploration, and as a result there will be an ongoing need for space life sciences core capabilities, including human-centered science, operations and engineering to mitigate the health and performance risk of human space flight.

Another assumption is in the longer term, there will be a greater focus on crew autonomy and increased human-robotics interaction as mission durations increase and are extended to travel to and on planets, and as a result, these is a continued need for research and development activity focused need for research and development activity focused on exploration risk reduction.

The next assumption is the pace of biomedical change will continue to be more rapid in external versus internal environments. Thus, solutions are more kinds of likely to be developed external to fight any different new unknown new diseases to attack to influence space people health to be poor , even cause death in possible.

What are space life science strategy goals?

On health innovation hands, the space exploration organization will drive advances in medical and environmental health for space flight in order to meet established space life standard and mission needs. Thus , innovation on medicine and biomedical / environment technology and processes will be developed, implement and incorporated into mission achievement.

On education hand, it needs to train in multidisciplinary life sciences, experts in exploration life science and that this is a continuous infusion of space ,life science into the public , government , academic and commercial sectors. Thus, the space life science education aim includes to teach the human system risk management, strategic relationship of any space missions, future space business model and space communication strategies.

The goal-specific strategies and measurable objectives can be developed for years 1 to 5 years It's objectives can include: optimize internal core capabilities throughout the planning cycle to enable the vision for space exploration with budgetary constraints, establish strategic relationship to achieve the full complement of life sciences capabilities necessary to be best in class , establish a center to integrate human health and performance efforts and expertise for space exploration worldwide, implement an internal and external communication plan to increase the life sciences value to encourage space human life education development for long term in commercial space flight sector.

Health innovation goal

Thus, one space exploration organization whose health innovation strategy is the main factor to influence its any overall space exploration missions inn success. Thus, it must need to spend more money and time and resource to ensure its health innovation implement can be succeed to reduce further every time space people's mission of physical illness or death or accident which are caused by space diseases . Thus, it will drive advances in medical and environmental health for space flight in order to meet establish space flight health standards and mission needs. Also, it needs to attempt to do any biomedical experiments to avoid space people who can contact to cause illness from any undiscovered space diseases.

Hence, the invention of space medicine, biomedical / space environmental technology and processes will be developed, implemented often every day/ IT needs to seek or gather every time practical space environment biomedical existing data and knowledge as a base for launching health technologies and to revise every time space biomedical experiment failure to find failure reasons to achieve the most absolute discovered any space unknown diseases biomedical experiment results. Thus, the improved methods and practice or recording data must concern to goals for human space exploration, attempting towards data gathering top continuing to achieve the best levels of evidence for answering operational and clinical questions regarding human health, safety and performance, during space flight and exploration and an evidence-based risk management approach to prioritize tasks.

The space biomedical experiments data gathering can consider human factors engineering, habitability design and human-robotics interaction will be recorded to analyze experiment result every time. These results will be developed, implemented and incorporated into mission architecture solutions to address the human as an element of the overall space system.

● Prediction on future trends in human space flight and future space human life science strategy relationship.

In the future, the relationship between future trends in human space flight and future space human life science will be more close. These reasons are that the trends in terrestrial life sciences will save as change drivers for space life sciences, include advanced in nano health, genetics, biocybernetics, self-constructing materials, human computer interfaces, medical and pharmaco-therapeutics, multi-scale physiological modelling and other biomedical technologies.

In conclusion, due to space exploration organization's objective is low tolerance for a risk and emphasis on risk quantification and reduction activities. Thus, the space human life science
strategy will be one important factors to cause any one space exploration organization's any missions in success.

● Why does Japan space organization consider space human life science?

Japan has acquired and advanced various space technologies. Through, these technologies level to allow to play a core role in the international human space activities . However, it's space exploration success is due to it concerns to achieve its space human life science strategy for its main point.

What social benefit from its utilization of the space environment to Japan. Because it concerns how to protect space human life during who are working in space. Thus, it can bring more social benefits to develop its space exploration industry for long term as below:

● Because it's space people can have health bodied, so who can attempt to any space science exploration experiments in space
environment as well as space human life science can raise Japan space people confidence to attempt to do every time space exploration activities in space environment. Consequently, they have confidence to catch rockets to go to space to gather various resource to do any space exploration to get research results more easily, which were achieved through utilization , such as micro gravity environment, that could not be produced on the ground, these outcomes include: protein crystal growth, that may lead to the development of new drugs, materials creation for next-generation semi-

conductors, and establishment of the technology for cubesats deployment, etc.

● Due to Japan space exploration organization concerns space people health issue. Thus, it has manned space flight capability can conduct youth development activities , with their own astronauts and such astronaut-led activities have aroused the younger generation's interest in outer space, taught them the importance of making efforts to making of one health space scientists confidence to pursue this space exploration industry.

Hence, when all Japan space scientists who own health bodies, then who can be one expansion of humankind's space of activities in this area create knowledge of planetary science and the quest of health space life and also contributes to the increase and accumulation of intellectual assets of all human beings.

The most reason of Japan's belief of space human life science strategy is very important , because it needs to prove human can live in space environment. Thus, if Japan's space scientists can have health bodies to do any space exploration experiments, then who is still health to go back Earth. Then , it proves the life support technologies , the space environment and health management and the maximum energy conservation. This leads to the enhancement of corporate brands and international appeal of technical capabilities , and is directly linked to resulting problems Japan faces , such as its aging population and lack of natural resources.

In conclusion, space human life science will influence Japan space exploration industry more success. Otherwise, if it chooses not to implement this space human life strategy. It won't have enough health space scientists to attempt to catch rockets to go to space to do any space exploration experiments more success in long term, e.g. seeking Earth another planets to provide Japan people to live, raising Japan young space scientists confidence to attempt to go to space to do any experiments because the Japan space exploration organization can provide new bio medical invention to supply when they are catching in the space rockets. If they feel that they are comfortable, they can eat or drink the new bio medical invention to avoid the space disease attack to cause their death or physical illness threat.

In conclusion, space human life science is very important factor to influence future every time human space exploration mission successfully.

Reference

Cater Iain , Carl 2010, " Steps to space: Opportunities for astro tourism development, tourism management 31 (2010); pp. 838-845; Elsevier Ltd, DOI: 10:1016/j.tourman. 2009.09.001

Collins Patric, Iwasaki Yoichi, Kanayama Hideki, Ohnuki Misuzo 1994, comercial implications of market research on space tourism. journal space technology and sciences , vol. 10 no 2, 94 Autumn, pp.3-11. copyright: Japanese rocket society; available at: www.spacefuture.com/archive/ commercial-implications-of market-research-on-space- tourism.shtml.

Collins Patric, Marita M; Stockmans R. and Kobayahi S. 1996. "Demand for space tourism in America and Japan and its implications for future space activities ". sixth international space conference of Pacific basic societies; Marina del rey; California: Advantages in the Astronautica science (AAS paper no AAS 95-605) vol. 91. pp. 601-610. Available at: http://m.internationalaerospaceconsulting.org/upload/space   % 20Future%20-%20Demand%   20for%20space%20Tourism%20in% 20America%20Japan.pdf

ESA 2008, " Richard Garriott, millionaire American space tourist. blasks off of international space station". published in 12.11.2008. Huffington post, seen on i01.04.2015; available at: http://www.huffington.com/2008/10/ 12/richard-garriott-milliona-n-1333940.html.

Klemm, G., & Markkanen, S. (2011). IN A Papathanassis (ed.) The long Tai , tourism (pp.95-103). Weisbaden, Germany : Gabler Verlag; Springer Fachmedien Weiesbaden GmbH.

KSCVC Visitors, 2013; MRI 2013 Market by Market

Von Der Dunk , F. (2012). The integrated approach. Regulating private human spaceflight as space activity, aircraft operation, and high-risk adventure tourism. Acta Astronautica, 92(2), 199-208.

Space Tourism Organization Strategy

Space tourism passengers leisure feeling

In future tourism leisure development, if we hope to develop our future space tourism entertainment in success, we need to know how to persuade general rich people how to make decision to choose to catch which kinds of rockets to travel outer space, because many of they will feel space is horror when they need to stay at the strange dark low degree temperature and none heavy weight body body feeling environment space environment. When they catch the rocket to visit the dark space strange environment.

In common, any space rocket passengers may usually feel dangerous , when their space rocket is crashed by any space stones suddenly. If one big size space stone flys toward to the space rocket direction to crash suddenly, due to the space rocket can not predict when any space stones will fly toward to this space rocket to crash it suddenly. Hence, space strange dark environment may influence many space tourism passengers feel fear to catch space rocket to fly in space environment in long time.

However, although flying to space environment toursim which may bring exciting and pleasure and enjoyment feeling to any one when they are catching the space rocket to fly to future space station, moon, even fly to space hotel to live one night or more, or stay the rocket to view our earth in different space environment locations for several minutes etc. different kinds of space tourism journeys. But, when the space rocket stays longer time in space environment, then it may bring more dangerous to the space rocket and the space passenger individual life both. Because many different kinds of space accidents may occur, e.g. space rocket has fire happens, machine equipment is damaged, space stones crash the rocket, space steel rubblishs crash the roctket, even space rocket windows may be damaged by any things etc. So, different kinds of accidents may be difficult to predict. Also, it implies that we may ensure any kinds of space rockets have chance to occur accidents when they are staying in the strange and dark space environment in any time.

Consequently, it will bring fear feeling to let any one space tourism passenger feel afraid to catch the space rocket to travel space long time. In special, if the space tourist is very rich, he must feel his life is value, he ought not lose his life due to this space rocket is crashed by any space stones, or space rubblishd ot itself damage factor etc. different space accidents occurrence. Hence, if any one space tourism service provider hopes that it can encourage many space tourists choose to catch itself space rocket in preference. It must need to let many its space rocket passengers feel itself space rocket is more safer or brings more safe feeling to let its all space rocket passengers to feel. Moreover, its needs to let many space tourism passengers may feel its space rocket is more safe to compare other space tourism leisure service providers their space rockets facilities.

Consequently, there are many space tourists may be influenced to choose to catch this space tourism lesiure service provider's space rocket to fly to space, because if they feel other space tourism leisure service providers , their space rockets are not safe to compare this space tourism leisure service provider's space rocket. Then, this space tourism leisure service provider may design different kinds of unique space journeys in order to let any space tourist feel more safe to stay longer time in space environment. Hence, it may help any one space leisure tourism service provider raise to charge higher ticket fee when its every space journey is longer time to compare general short time space journeys.

Is right time to develop space tourism lesiure

Nowadays, human can have different kinds of lesiure choices. They may include tourism in ourselves earth, sports, visiting cinemas to see movies, listening musics, reading ebooks or paper books, visitng theatre to see art performances, seeing paints etc. any every different kinds of lesiure activities. However, comparing among of any kinds of general lesisures, tourism lesiure must be the most expensive kind of entertainment activity to compare all of above these different kinds of lesiure activities. Hence, it brings this question: Is right time to develop space tourism leisure market?

In fact, future human travel choice has only these both kinds: One is travelling in ourselves earth, another is catching rocket to travel space, e.g. visiting space station, staying on space one location to view ourselves earth or moon, or visiting moon, living space hotel one night or more etc. different kinds of space tourism leisure activities. However, I beleive that it is right time to develop space tourism leisure. I shall explain as below:

The first reason, all of us ought know that this kind of disease COVID 19 had influenced global many travellers had began to feel fear to catch air planes to go to other countries to travel because many travellers began to believe that they may get this kind of illness easily when any one of air plane passengetr is sitting close to the COVID 19 patient, even any one air plane passenger may also be gotten by air when any one COVID 19 patient is sitting in the close window air plane seat. Hence, COVID 19 disease is significant to influence global many travellers began to reduce to catch any air planes to go to any countries to travel frequently, even the having travelling habit travellers will choose not travelling any countries any times by air planes.

So, it seems that COVID 19 disease will have long time to influence futuer global tourism leisure market development in our earth. It is one negative psychological factor of " feeling afraid to catch air plane" to any one liking tourism leisure tourist. So, when one likes often to go to other countries to travel, in special, the high income or rich people group, when they feel fear to need to catch air planes to go to other countries to travel, they must feel bore, due to they must only stay in themselves home countries by COVID 19 disease attacks. In fact, although these high income or rich people tourist group can choose any kinds of leisures to replace tourism leisure activity, e.g. sport, going to cinemas to see movies, going to concert halls to listen musics or songs, going to theatres to see art performances. But, all of these different kinds of entertainment activities can not satisfy themselves leisure psychological needs, because they have much money, they like to spend money to go to any countries to travel for one week, or two weeks , even one month more in their holidays.

Nowadays, because this kind of COVID 19 disease influences they feel afraid to catch air planes to travel to any countries frequently. They avoid to catch air planes to contact any one, he/she may have COVID 19 diease, even when they arrive the traveling destination, they none COVID 19 disease travellers , they feel that their bodies may be goten COVID 19 disease, when they need visit any one hotel to rent rooms to live, or rent appartments to live, they must need to live strange hotel room. However, the hotel room may be lived by any one COVID 19 patient, when the tourist choose to live the hotel room, he will have chance to get COVID 19 disease due to he contact any things in the hotel room. Even, any one tourist needs to catch any train, bus, tram, taxi, ferry , underground train etc. different kinds of public transport tools, they may have chance to get COVID 19 disease when they are catching the public transport tool, if it has any one COVID 19 disease passenger is catching the same bus or other kinds of public transport tool, or they need to go to any one restaurants to eat breakfasts, lunchs, or dinners, they need to sit the table with the COVID 19 patient together, ot they need to walk on the streets or they need to climb mountains or they need to visit any travelling destinations etc. to do any kinds of travelling leisure activities, that they need to do in their travelling jounrneys. So, it implies that they have chance to bring COVID 19 disease to themselves bodies due to they have chance to contact any one strange person in any travelling destinations. Hence, they will feel that they may be contacted to get COVID 19 disease , when they are staying in the travelling country.

Consequently, it seems that COVID 19 siease may be one important factor to influenc global any one feels afraid to catch air planes to go to anywhere to travel. SO, such as the special rich travellers group, they only have another travel choice to replace tourism in earth, it is " visiting space tourism". Although , every tecket for any one kind of space tourism , it may be very expensive, but for this special rich traveller groups, their space tourism leisure needs ought not be influenced reduce by expensive ticket factor easily. Because they feel that space tourism will be only another kind of expensive lesiure activity to replace tourism leisure in our earth.

The another reason is that global rich people number had been increasing every year significant. For China and US and UK and India etc. these high population countries, their rich people number had been climbed countinue every year . Hence, it implies that future many people have effort to epend at least one time of space tourism leisure, due to rich people number had been increasing in countinue. Moreover, many habit travellers began to feel that our earth has none any value destinations to visit, when they had visited any one travelling destinations at least one time. So, when many travellers feel that they had attempted to visit any vaue travelling destinations, then they won't like to buy air ticket to visit any one of these travelling destinations again. So, the only one tourism choice, is that visiting to space 's any destinations, e.g. visiting moon, visiting space stations to live one night hotel hotel, staying on space one location to vire ourselves earth or moon etc. different kinds of space journeys. Because may of rich travellers had felt that travelling in oursleves is low valur leisure and it can not attract any one rich tourist chooses this kind of lesiure again, as well as they had felr that earth has none any destinations can attract them to travel, so it is only space tourism may replace tourism in ourselves earth.

On conclusion, it is right time to prepare to invest another new kind of tourism leisure, such as space tourism , it may repalce traditional tourism in earth leisure. SO developing space tourism leisure is one value leisure developing market.

CHAPTER FIVE

Can technology development influence space tourism development

Human Behavioral network job brings social economic benefits

What does human network job mean ? Why may human network job be popular? Why human network job behavior may influence economy ? Nowadays internet is popular to use. We can apply internet to find data , search any new things, even earn money. Why does internet
may become huma network job source. For example, e-publish may be one kind of new human network job. Any authors may apply internet
channel to help them to sell electronic or paper books from e-publisher web store. They may apply facebook, you tub etc. any online
channel to promote themselves new books to let new readers to know whether when they may buy themselves favourable new topic books to read

from electronic publisher web store.

Thus, future electronic publisher industry may help any authors to build internet network platform to help them to sell and promote
ot advertise their any one new electronic or paper book topic to let global any one reader to choose to buy their any new topic books from electronic publisher web store easily and conveniently. However, it implies that electronic network platform author may be one kind of future new human network job in our societies.

How electronic network platform author job may bring economy benefit in macro economy view? A person can have few friends, contacts and still be very influential if these few friends and contacts are themselves highly influential, e.g. one author must not need to know any one reader in global society. When they like to choose any electronic books from electronic internet network platform. They may become the author's any one topic book buyer, when they feel the author's any one topic book is fun and attract they make decision to buth the strange author whose the topic book from electronic book publisher's platform web store conventiently in short time. Although, they are strangers, they do not know themselves , but the reader can understand what it way that made Google from writing platofrm to create new creative mind and typing network job method to replace traditional hand writing book method for global authors. It will be one kind of new human network writing job.

Hence, global any one reader can apply an innovative search engine , such as google.com to find whether whom author personal new topic books are value to read from internet.

Then, the electroniuc publisher's web store may be new book store platform sale network to help the author to sell many electronic or paper books from electronic network platform

in short time. So, internet may be future new network plaform to help global any one author to create network writing job absolutely. Furthermore, internet may be popular social media

to help any one author to build goold relationship between his/her readers. It is one kind of new network, human network job. New authors do not need to buy many paper books to prepare to put in any one book shop warehouse. Their every book can print on demand to reduce out of book stock in any one book shop. They may choose to sell either electronic books or paper books both from any one book publisher web store. So, electronic network platform may be one kind of good writing channel to help human authors to create income and it can also help authors to bring new creative mind and new topic fun content books to let readers to know and buy to read from electronic publisher network platform.

Why does human behavior may be one kind of new human network job to bring global economic advantages. ALthough, it may be free income or without inocme, but the person does the network behavior, his/her behavior may be bring advantages to influence many other people's health. For this case, when a worker in a coffee shop in an airport gets a vaccination againnst the flu, it does not only helps him or her stay healthy, but also helps the many travellers who might otherwise have been inflected if that workers caught the flu. So, the externality , the result implies the vaccination of even a part of a community conveys benefits to the whole community. For example, governments pay special attention to the vaccinations of school children, teachers, health mothers, and the elderly, categories of people particularly susceptible not only to catching, but also to transmitting a disease.

It is not accidential that governments are heavily involved with vaccination . When there are externalities, free market, fail to persuade individual incentives with society's

their the worker's decision of whether to get a vaccine ends up attracting whether other people get sick. The workers might not fully take all these other people's potential suffering into account when making her or his vaccination decision.

As Stanford University does many suggestions, understand this and tries to help them make the right decisions and so providers free flu vaccines for its staff and students.

Small pockets of unvaccinated individuals can allow a disease to gain a spread more widely well-being. For example, parent weighing the costs and benefits of a vaccine for their child is not always thinking of the consequences of that vaccination to other people. THese are markets in which subsidizing or regulating behavior can make everyone better off. Because the reason for requiring that a child be vaccinated before enrolling in school is not just to protect that child, because each child's vaccination affects others via potential contagions.

Robots take our jobs behavioral and economy influences

Robot job behavior brings economy influences

If one day robots can replace human to do simple, even complex jobs. They will bring what influences to our global societial economy.The popular economic refrain declares that the

global middle class is dying and robots will soon take our jobs, e.g. shopping center customer service jobs, library service jobs, cinema ticket sale jobs, restaurant kitchen cooker jobs,

even, bus drivers, taxi drivers etc. public transport driving jobs, accountant, doctors etc. professional jobs. Whether it is beautiful or petty matter if our future societies have many human jobs can be replaced to do from robots. Businessman must may reduce to employ employees and reduce to pay salary or wage, when robots can be replaced to do their employees tasks. But, societies must bring unemployement rate rises , due to societies will have many people loss jobs when their employers choose to buy robots to serve their clients or do any office tasks or customer service or cleaning etc. tasks.

In micro economy view, employers may save money in long term, but in macro economy view, it will cause unemployment ratio rises , even crime rate rises when there are many people lose
jobs in societies. These models of doom, though, fail to account for the hundreds of businesses riding the waves of change in their industries when robots may be invented to replace human to do many simple , even complex tasks in our future societies.

WE may image that one small factory needs to manufacture fishes canes to sell to supermarket, the small , cheaper stuff and higher margin parts of the fishes manufacture industry. Before, this factory needs to employe many human factory workers need to help every fresh customer makeing the perfect fishing gear, designed for performance, durability, and cost in order to achieve to manufacture every fish cane in whole fished processing manufacturing stages. Every worker needs to spend about 15 to twenty minutes to finish every fish cane , till to delivery to any supermarket to sell. If this fish canes manufacturing factory can apply manufacturing robots to help them to finish any one working tasks , every robot can only spend five minutes to finish whole fresh fish cane manufacturing process. Thus, every robot can
help this factory save 10 to 15 minutes time to finsh every fish cane manufacturing process. IN fact, time is money, because when every robot can help this factory to reduce 10 to 15 minutes time to compare human worker. Then, this factory can finish about 20 fish canes in one hour if it can use robot to help it to manufacture fish canes. Otherwise, if this factory still use human workers to help it to manufacture fish canes, then it can finsh about 3 to 4 fish canes in one hour. SO, the manufacturing efficiency ensures that robots must help this fish manufacturing factory to raise fish canes number more than human workers. So, in robotic behavioral economy view, manufacturing robots must help this fish canes manufacturing factory to raise fish canes manufacturing number and deliver increasing number to supermarkets to prepare to sell every day. Robots can help this fish canes manufacturing factory bring manufacturing time saving, rising manufacturing efficiency, improving performance and reducing wages expenditure long time advantages in micro economy view. However, manufacturing robots can also bring disadvanages to society, e.g. increasing

unemployment ratio, increasing crime rate,

this factory workers will lose jobs and income, they need earn social welfare from government and increasing government finance pressure in short time, even long time in macro economic view.

Stanford University graduate program in economics, Scott lecturer explained that "in demand and supply economic theory for robots supply and demand case, robots supply number increasing may influence human workers demand number decrease. It sometimes calls " the efficient frontier".

No specific human beings were mentioned in any of economics classes. As robots supply and demand in market case, They (robots) may be purely theoretical " agents" who reached to the most reasonable sale prices in order to persuade any one businessman buyer to make manufacturing robot buying decision whether robots can help him / her to bring how much saving time , saving money, saving cost, improving performance, efficiency economic benefit before he/she plans to reduce workers number when he/ she decides to apply robots to replace human workers in his/her factory or office or any service department, e.g. cinema ticket sale service, shopping center customer service, shopping center cleaning , supermarket customer service etc. service or sale tasks. When robots can replace human to do any one of these tasks in any organizations. So, robots may be human worker agents who reached to prices the way robots would react to a software

command. There was nothing that explained why some people thrived and others did n't or why truly brilliant, hardworking people could fail when much lazier folks succeeded." Having been admitted to the Stanford University graduate program in economics, Scott lecturer hoped to get his answers there.

How robots influence our future social changing? Using the right technology can be a boon to your business in this economy. For internet example, it is easier than ever to find well-matched customers all around the world, to stay in contact with them, and to more quickly design the products they want. If you focus solely on being cutting -edge, though you risk letting the technology

take over what should be very robust relationships with your customers , employees, and colleagues. IN nowaddays society, technoligical advances and cutomation, personal

relationships in business are more crucial than ever. I mean that robots can not replace human to serve clients to let them to feel more comfortable and passion more easily. For shoe shop case example, if the shoe shop apply one robot to serve its clients to replace human shoe salesperson to serve its shoe customers. Robots ensure that they can not persuade every shoe potential buyer to make shoe buying decision more easily when robots need to contact every shoe potential buyer. The reason is simple, because robots can not touch any one shoe buyer individual emotion very easier.

If the shoe buyer needs the robots to help him/her to choose any right shoe styles when he/she can not feel himself / herself can make the most right shoe style choice decision. The robots can not replace human shoe salesperson to make shoe style choice judgement more easily. They must need longer time to analyze whether which shoe style may be the most suitable to the shoe buyer. Otherwise, human shoe salesperson may attempt to make the most right shoe style choice decision to help any one shoe buyer to chooce the most right style shoe because he/she owns shoe style sale experience, shoe style knowledge, the most important reason is that they can feel every shoe customer individual emotion to touch whether he/she will feel comfortable or happy when they attempt to help every shoe customer to seek the most right shoe style in every shoe customer whole shoe searching processing. Othwerwise, serving robots are only one machine, they can not touch or feel every shoe customer individual emotion whether he/she feel comfortable or unhappy or happy when they need to contact them in whole shoe searching processing. Hence, I believe that some tasks robots can

not repalce human staff to do very easily. Otherwise, robots may bring disadvanatges to let any one businessman to loss his/her customers, due to robots can not touch every customer

emotion to compare human staff in service tasks more easily. Robots serving customer behaviors may cause money lose and customers number lose to the shop in micro economic view.

Intellectual human economic behaviors

What does intellectual human economic behaviors mean ? I believe that when we choose or decide to do intellectual behaviors, then our societies will be influenced to bring economic growth in consequence.I shall attempt to indicate pollution case to explain how and why eithet our intellectual or foolish behaviors may bring economic growth or recession in consequence as below:

On one hand, for air pollution social case aspect example, if we only consider to buy cars to drive for working aimr or holiday leisure aim. Then, our societies air will be polluted. Our health will be influenced to bad. Our car driving behaviors may cause global environment air pollution serously. In long tiem, global air pollution will bring our bodies health to be bad. Although, ourselves car driving behaviors may bring our driving travelling leisure enjoyment and comfortable feeling in short time, also we so not need to pay public transport fare often, but we need to compensate ourselves health economic intangible loss due to air pollution , when cars number increases, dirty air will cause ouselves health to become bad.

In the result, we will need to pay more medical expenditure when we are old age, due to ourselves bodies will become bad, due to we breathe global dirty air every day, due to ourselves cars pollute air in long time, e.g. 10 to 20 years, even 30 more without limited air pollution environment. So, driving cars behavior may be one kind of human foolish behavior and our foolish behavior may bring ourselves future long time medical expenditure absolutely.

One the other hand, water pollution social aspect, if we often keep much rubblish to pollute sea, oil exploration porcessing pollute ocean , ships gas pollute ocaen, then fishes will eat polluted food and drive dirty water, due to global ocean is polluted.

In fact, because human only to conside how to buy boats to carry on leisure enjoyment activities, or catch cruises to travel on the sea. Also, oil manufacturers only consider researching anywhere to find new oil exploration places to manufacture oil product, when their oil exploration processes pollute ocarn . Consequently, global fishes drink polluted warer or eat polluted food. They will have poison. SO, human will have high chance to eat poison polluted fishes, due to fishes are poison or are polluted.

So, human is doing foolish activities, we only hope to find oil exploration places to pollute ocean or we only spend money to buy ticket to catch ships to travel anywhere in global ocean. All of these human foolish behaviors will bring pollution to global ocean. On consequently, we will need to compensate to eat polluted or dirty or poision fishes, ourselves bodies health will be bad. In long time, we need have high chance to pay medical expenditure when we are old. So, pollution case may be one good example to explain how and why human foolish behavior may influence ourselves future need to compensate serious medical loss.

All of these human foolish behavior will bring pollution to global ocean. On consequently, we will need to compensate to eat polluted or dirty or poison fished , ourselves bodies health will be bad. In long time, we will have high chance to pay medical expenditure, when we are old. So, pollution case may be one good example to explain how and why human ourselves intellectual or foolish behaviors may influence future long time economic loss or economic growth or recession in micro and micro economic view.

On another water pollution aspect hand, if we often keep rubbish to sea, oil exploration processing pollutes ocean and ships' gas pollute ocean, then fishes will eat polluted food and drink dirty water, due to fishes will eat polluted food and drink dirty sea water because the global ocean is polluted seriously.

In fact, because human only consider how to buy boats to carry on any leisure water activities, or catches cruises to travel on the sea. Also, oil manufacturers only consider any where to find oil exploratin places to manufacture oil products from ocean, when their pol exploration processes can plooute ocean. Consequently, global fishes drink polluted water or eat direty food. They will have poison. So, human will have high chance to eat poison fishes.

Otherwise, such as pollutin case, it can infuence inflation or deflation. Consequently, the reason indicates supply and demand theory. If air pollution is serious, then we will consider health issue, global cars demand number may be influenced to reduce, when global cars number demand will reduce, global car prices and supply number will need to change to fall down in order to attract or persuade global car consumers choose to make car purchase decision.

Hence, global car manufacture number and car price will be influenced to reduce, due to global air pollution issue. Consequently, deflation will occur because when the country citizen usually does not spend much extra saving money to buy car expensive goods. Money value will be low. Otherwise, if global cair pollution is not serious, human considers to buy cars to enjoy driving leisure lives. So, global car demand is influenced to increase , also global car price will also influenced to increase.

Consequently, gobal human will choose to buy cars to drive. Due to we accept to spend extra saving to buy expensive car goods. Car sale price and supply may be influenced to rise up. Money value is influenced to reduce. Inflation may be influenced, due to global car consumers number increases, we would not have extra money to spend easily. Car expensive goods expenditure influences our spending habit to avoid to make car purchase decision more easily. So, human intellectual or foolish activities may bring inflation or deflation consequency in possible indirectly in macro economic view.

On conclusion, above pollution case explain that how and why human intellectual or foolish economic behaviors may bring inflation or deflation consequency as wll as economic growth or recession consequency as well as any goods demand and supply increasing or decreasing consequency. It implies that human behavior may have indirect relationship to influence any goods demand and supply number to either increase or decrease result as well as any goods price will be influenced to increase or decrease in micro and macro economic view.

The relationship between social change and human behavior

Why does economic changes may influence human individual behavioral change? I shall attempt to indicate shopping behavior and staying at home behavior to explain their case and effect relationsip as below:

Human behavior can be influenced by economic change or economic change can be influenced by human behavior? Why does recession may influence consumers reduce shopping desire? In social recession suitation, it is possible that many people lose jobs suddenly, due to businessmen lose many customers. They need to make decision to reduce employees number in order to continue to keep businesses. Consequently, many firms (organizations) their employees may lose jobs. When they have much time, due to lose jobs, they will feel to avoid to spend too much time and money to go to shopping often. Many losing jobs people, they will often stay at homes. So, they will reduce time to go to shopping, then non essential products won't their preferable choice purchase products. Hence, recession will change many losing jobs people their shopping or consumption desires to avoid to buy non essential products often . Usually when economic boom, many people have jobs to do because consumers number must increase when many people have jobs to do. Then, many people can accept to spend money to buy non essential products often. Many people feel spend time to go to shopping can satisfy their purchase of any kinds of new products useful psychology or desire. So, recession is one good example to explain it can influence many people do not like often to leave homes to go to shopping easily. Many people like to stay at homes, becaue they feel worry about spending too much shopping time when they leave homes. Their staying home time is one good negative shopping behavior example. So, economic change may influence human individual behavior changes , they have direct cause and efect relationsip in behavioral economic view.

May human behavior influence economic change? Is it possible that human behavior may bring the country social economic change in macro economic or micro behavioral economic view ? I shall indicate publishing industry example. Do you feel that if there are many students feel learning is very important when they read many books or many of students feel interesting to read or they have reading new books in habit, then it is possible that the country will have many students like to spend time to go to any book shops to choose the books, they feel that they can help they learn new knowledge. Then the country will increase students number, they often spend time to visit any one book shop every week. Their visiting book shops behavior which may become their habits. So, the country will increase students number, they often spend time to visit book shops. Also, it implies that visiting book shops behaviors may be their behavioral habits.

So, when the country has many students often spend time to visit book shops , their visiting book shops behaviors may help any one book shop to raise books sale chance. So, the country's student individual often visiting book shop behaviors, their habitual visiting book shops behaviors must may assist help any one book shop to increase books sale number absolutely.

Consequently, any one book shop , its books sale bumber must be influenced to increase to increase because the country will have many students like or feel need visit book shops habit in order to choose any suitable books to buy to read at home in order to raise themselves learning effort. When the country has many bok shops often have many students visit their book shops, then their books sale number may be influenced to increase. It explain why student individual visiting book shop behavior may help any one book shop sale number increases also.

How human productive behavior may influence economic development

May any country which citizen behavior assist themselves country development? It is one cause and effect economic question. I mean that if the country itself citicen can not concentrate mind or energy to choose to do one kind of industry in order to let themselves country can bring the most benefit, then whether the counry itself economy can bring the most serious economic benefit. I shall attempt to indicate these countries themselves indistry choice to explain whether these countries themselves citizen productive behavior may help themselves countries to achieve the largest economic benefits. I shall indicate as below:

New Zealand farmer individual wine productive behavior

For New Zealand country example, this country concerns itself effort is foucs on farming agricultural aspect. So, this country has many farmers concentrate on farming agricultural aspect. May New Zealanders choose to spend time to produce different kinds of wines, e.g. wine or red grape wine is for the people are eating meat, or they are eating dinner.

When these New Zealanders their behaviors choose to do farming or agriculture to grow and produce different kinds of taste of white or red grape wine drinking products job. Themselves grape agriculture behavior will influence these New Zealanders themselves, they can learn how to improve different kinds of grape wine drinking products in order to achieve every kinds of white or read grape wines taste improving aim during their white or red grape producing process.

Why can New Zealander every individual white or read grape wine producers improve their white or read grape wine taste more easily? In behavioral economic view, it can explain that why any one New Zealander white or read grape wine producer can be encouraged or excited or persuaded to concentrate nervous and energy and effort to learn how to improve their white or red grape wine products easily.

In fact, New Zealand is one agricultural food export country. It has good natural environment resource , e.g. land, seed to provide any one farmer to produce themselves any kinds of agricultrual food products, e.g. fruit, or wine food products. Because New Zealanders know themselves country has enough natural resource . So, in common, many New Zealanders choose to attempt to do farming agricultural jobs in order to export themselves any kinds of fruit or meat or wine products to overseas or sell to domestic in order to earn profit.

So, when these New Zealand farmers number has been increasing every year. This country farmers will feel themsleves competition between this New Zealand farmers themselves are serious due to they may feel New Zealanders choose to do agriculture businesses in order to export themselves different kinds of farming food to overseas or sell to local to earn profit.

Hence, when many New Zealand farmers feel that farmers number has been increasing every year. They will feel themselves competition is serious. They must need to spend much time and nervous and effort to research what method is the best how to produce the best taste of white or red grape wine products in order to let local or overseas wine buyers to choose to buy his/her producing white or read grpae products to drink.

Hence, in competition psychological view, may influence many New

Zealand white or reaad wine producers had been beginning to change their learning behavior on researching what method is the best in order to produce the best quality of taste red or white wine products to sell in order to attract overseas or local white or read grape wine drinkers to choose to buy his/her wine products. Their behavior will focus on learning how to raising or improving white or read grape wine taste method more than only focus on producing a large number white or red grape wine products. They believe wine quality is more important to compare wine producing number. So, New Zealand wine producers themselves wine producers behaviors have been changing on concentrating on researching wine quality method aspect more then wine producing number aspect in behavioral economic view.

America high technological productive behavior
For America example, US is one high technological country, it owns many high technological knowledge talent inventors, e.g. computer science inventors. Hence, US must attract many diferent countries owning high technological computer inventors choose to go to US to develop their computer science profession career. Also, it seems that when many computer science inventors or professions choose to go to US to develop themselves computer science new career. In behavioral economic view, due to their leaving themselves countries choice, which may bring influence themselve country job behaviors need to be changed. They must need to adapt US new live. Because they will forgive their past computer science job. These computer science professionals need to spend time to adapt US new lives. They " past computer science job behaviors" will need to be changed to their new US any computer employer's new computer science job model.
Because their traditional computer science jobs needed to be forgot in their themselves countries. They will feel their old computer science job knowledge and behavior needed to change in order to let their US any one new of computer company employer feels satisfactory to accept their new working behavior in any one US computer organization.
So, on the other hand, many US computer company employer will feel that they must need time to accept any one new overseas computer science professions their working behaviors, their working attitude daily, because these foreign comouter science professional, their past computer working behaviors and working attitude must be different to US domestic computer science professions.

In behavioral economic view, these overseas computer science professions, their working behaviors and attitude must be needed to change in order to adapt any one US new computer company itself domestic or local computer science professional stafs themselves daily working behaviors and attitude because these overseas and local computer science professionals must need to team work together.

In behavioral economic view, it is only one way that foreign computer science professionals must need to change themselves past country traditiona daily working behaviors and attitude in order to cooperate with these US local computer science professionals in teams more easily.

Consequently, if these foreign compute science professionals can change their past working behaviors and attitude to let any one US local computer science professional feels to cooperate with them easily in short time. Then, the US computer company itself whole computer professional teams themselves efficiencies will be influenced to raised or improved by the changing past working attitude and working behaviors of these foreign computer science professionals. So, in behavioral economic view, only if US any one computer company hopes itself computer teams themselves efficiency can be raised or improved when it decides to employ foreign computer science professionals and US domestic computer science professionals. They need to work in teams together. They must need to let these foreign computer science professionals to know how to change their working behaviors and attitude to let their domestic computer science professionals feel easy to work together. Then, the US computer company itself whole team efficiency must be rasied or improved easily in short time.

● China share market investing behavior

For China share market example, economic development depends on financial market. Because if many Chinese have interest to invest to carry on shares buying and selling activities in orde to learn how to earn shares interest and share profit when the China shareholder can make decision to sell himself/herself shares in the the high price, then he/she can earn money when he/she can sell the China company's shares in the high sale share price position.

If China has many Chinese like to spend time to carry on investing shares activities. Themselves shares buying and selling behaviors will influence China has many companies can increase fund from many Chinese shareholders in order to have enough money to expand or develop themselves businesses in China in long term.

Consequently, when China can have many Chinese like to attempt to carry on buying and selling shares investing behaviors in China share market. Themselves buying and selling shares behaviors can help many Chinese companies have effort to increase enough money or capital in order to continue to do their businesses in long term absolutely. So, it explains why when many Chinese become shareholders , they can assist China will have many companies continue to develop their businesses if many Chinese like to carry on shares buying and selling investing behaviors in long time in China financial investment market nowadays in behavioral economic view.

Why has any individual country have many people invest share behavior which can influence the country's macro consumption desire?
I shall apply shares market buying and selling investment behavior to explaiin why shares investment behavior which may impact the country's overal consumption desire as below:
In behavioral economic view, I assume that when the coutry has many people have interest to attempt to carry on shares buying and selling investment behavior, then their frequent shares buying and selling behaviors which may bring negactive consumption desire or shopping desire of these shares investors their consumer behavior.
The reason is simple, when the country has many share buyers number suddenly been increasing rapidly. Consequently, these large group share investors must need to spend much time to research any kinds of company shares variations, whether when their share prices will rise up of fall down in order to achieve buying the company's shares in the lowest price and selling the company's shares in the highest price level in order to earn profit.
Basic on this reason, they must need to spend much extra time to research share prices changing behavior every day, e.g. one working person will wait to leave his/her job, after he/she can spend time to gather data to research the day's share price changing behavior after dinner. So, the working person's right time may be his/her share price market research behavior. Before he/she may spend his/her night time to go to shopping after dinner, but nowadays, he/she will fogive to do his/her shopping behavior before dinner or after dinner at hight sometime. He/she will make decision to spend much night time to turn on computer to click on share market website to research his/her share purchase choice to investigate whether his/her share price whether it rises up or falls down at the moment in order to make his/her share buying or selling decision at ever night time.

I mean the when the country has many people are share investors, their shares investment behavioral spenging time which will influence many shops lose customers at might often because the country will have many people feel need to spend night time to turn on computer or watch television to investigate share price variation. So, the country will have many people / share investors choose to stay at home in order to carry on share price variation investigation behavior, they need to listen share market update news from radios or watch the share market update news from computer or TV at home every night. Consequenly, they must reduce times to leave themselves homes at night. So, their shopping behavior also will be reduced. Because these share investors feel need to spend time to investigate share price variation news at homes which can bring economic benefits (high opportunity benefits) when they choose to forgive to leave homes to go to shopping times (opportunity cost) every night.

On conclusion, it seems that when the country has many people are share investors, then their share price investigating behavior may bring negative shopping emotion at night. Consequently, the country's any one shop may lose many customers from this share investor consumer group in behavioral economic view. Hence, when the country's share investors number had been increasing rapidly, it will influence any shops lose many customers from this share investing customer group at night frequenly in short time, even long time in behavioral economic view, because their shopping desires or shopping emotion will be brought negative feeling when they make decisions to spend much time to listen radios or watch TV or computers share price update nes at night. Hence, share market will bring negative impact to influence consumer shopping desire or negative shopping emotion in behavioral economic view.

Can technology influence human shopping behavioral change?
Nowadays, technological development has reached mature stage, whether technological mature stage may bring positive or negative shopping emotion influence to global consumers. I shall aplly internet inventin or ecommerce shopping channel tool to explain whether internet technology can bring postive or negative influence to global consumer behavior in behavioral economic view.

Internet is a good technological tool, it brings e-commerce business chance. In fact, commonly, global has have many businessmen choose to use internet channel to carry on their products transactions between global online-buyers and their electronic websites. So, global many shoppers had begun to feel online shopping is more convenient to compare visiting shops shopping. Their shopping behaviors have been changed from internet technological tool. Global has many shoppers choose to buy any products from any overseas or local businessmen their web stores. They only need to spend time to find any businessmen their webstores to choose the most suitable products to pay visa to buy from their webstores. at homes. So, in general, global had have may shoppers had changed their shopping behaviors from visiting shops to visiting webstores at homes often.

So, it seems that internet technological tool had influenced global many shops disappear, but internet webstores will be replaced their actual shops on streets. Some of businessmen either they choose webstores to replace shops or choose websotes and shops both or still keep shops only. Hence, internet tool influences global businessmen have three kinds of products sale channels to let globa local and overseas consumers to choose how to buy their products.

However, in fact, many of global shoppers, youngers and olders had begun to accept to buy any products from webstores. They feel to spend time to leave homes to visit shops , their shopping behaviors will be wasted time to not essential part to their daily lives. Hence, since internet technological invention, it had changed many consumers their traditional visiting shops shopping habit to change to buying products from webstores channel.

However, on the one hand, internet creates webstores ecommerce shopping channel to let global many consumers do not need to leave homes to go to shopping. It brings negative visiting shops shopping emotion to global general consumers nowadays. But on the other hand, it also brings positive visiting internet webstores shopping emotion to global general consumer nowadays. So, it seems that global many consumers feel that they often do not need to spend much time to go out shopping. Many global consumers feel convenient and enjoy to choose any products to buy from different internet webstores, when the online buyer chooses the most suitable product, he she only needs to pay visa card to buy the product from the online seller's webstore conveniently at home.

Hence, online shopping can bring economic benefit to online buyers, e.g. avoiding walking time or spending transport fare to visit the shop to go to shopping, shortening or reducing shopping time to do another important matter.

On conclusion, global many consumers began feel online shopping can bring more economic benefits on shortening shopping time, avoiding transport fare spending aspect. So, online shopping will be popular shopping behavior for future long time. It may encourage global many shoppers can make rapid shopping decision in short time in order to carry on any products buying transaction to global any one online shopper in short time easily in behavioral economic view. So, global many businessmen had begun to build themselves one attraction webstore in order to persuade different countries consumers to choose to click themselves webstores from internet channel to buy any kinds of products in short time easily.

So, internet technology had changed consumers traditional shopping behaviors to build positive online shopping emotion as well as raise online sellers' any products sale chance easily in behavioral economic view.

Why and how human behavior may influence the country's economic growth or recession?

When one country has many people choose to do the same matter for one period, whether their behavior may influence the country's pvera; economic growth or recession . I shall attempt to indicate cases toexplain their relationship as below:

For flowing rubblish behavioral case example, do you feel that when the country has many people often flow rubblish on the streets, instead of their flowing rubblish behavior may bring streets dirty? But, their flowing rubblish behavior may explain that this country has people may have enough money to buy food to ear, or enough cloths to wear, enough bottles of water to drink, even they may have enough money to buy new television, radio, refrigeraters , washing machines, desktops or laptops electronic home products from old to new to use in order to satisfy their living needs. So, when they flow old electronic home products, their flowing old home electronic products behaviors may seem that they have enough money to buy other new home electronic products to replace old home electronic products to use at homes.

However, it seems thaat this country ought have many people have jobs to do. So, many of them, they can easy to make purchase decison to flow any old home electronic products and buy any new home electronic products to use . Because this country has many people have jobs to do. So, they can often not use old home electonic products to become rubblishs to flow on streets after they had bought any kinds of new home electronic homes.

In fact, it also implies that this country's economy grows rapidly. So, many businesses can glow up rapdly. When they expanded their businesses, they must need to increase employees number in order to let they help themselves to raise productivity or serve their clients absolutely. So, when the country has many businesses can grow up, it seems that its economy must be better or it is improved to compare past. Due to many different kinds of home electronic products had been often bought to use by this country people in this period. So, this country's any streets can be observed that expensive electronic home products were flowed on streets anywhere. then, this country will have many electronic home products sellers can sell their home electronic products very easily. When this country has many people can find any kinds of jobs to do easily. So, due to unemploymen rate had been decreasing.

In behavioral economic view, as this many electronic home products rubblish country case, we can observe this country may have many people have jobs to do. So, consumption number has been increased long time. So, cheap food, or expensive home electronic products may be rubblish on any streets. This country's people , their flowing rubblish behaviors may be explained that many of people have enough jobs to do, so they have ability to buy any good taste food to eat or buy any kinds of expensive electronic home products to use. So, this country's economy may be improved for this long period. So, in behavioral economic view, when this country can have many electronic home products rubblishs are flowed on anywherer in streets frequently. It seems that this country will have many people have jobs to do, so it causes they often change old home electronic products or replaced them easily, when they have enough income to spend to buy any kinds of new home electronic products to use at homes easily. Moreover, their flowing old electronic home products behaviors also indicate that this country has many people their salaries may be increased in possible from their emplyers. When this country can have many different kinds of home electornic products are sold. It means that this country's electronic home products needs or demand had been increasing, due to many people have jobs to do and income increases to excite their living of needs also improve. Consequently, this country may seem have better economic improvement. We can observe from this country's electronic home products rubblish increasing income in theis period.

On conclusion, this country ought experience economic growth at this period. So, " flowing expensive electronic home rubblish increasing number " may seem that this country's economic growth is rapidly in this period, due to many people have jobs to do as well as salaries increase in this period.

Technology how impacts human behavior changing?

Technology how influences human behavior to bring changing? For example, online share purchase and sale transaction from smart phone brings share investor can do share buying or selling transation in any where and any time conveniently, non manual driving auto vehicle, bring car owner feels comfortable and spends free time to do other matter, e.g. reading, listening mucis in himself or herself car freely. electrical energy vehicle can help car owner to reduce air polluton and it can brings the drivers do not feel drive long time in any journeys in order to avoid air pollution for environmental protection responsible car drivers in our societies. Thus, they will drive long time in any journeys when they can drive electronic energy cars to replace oil energy cars.

However, online technology can also bring consumers can choose to stay at homes to buy any things from seller individual online webstore conveniently. Such as online technology can bring shoppers do not need to spend much time to visit shops to buy any things. They can choose any kinds of products from any online sellers individual online webstores conveniently at homes. Online technology excite busy consumers can make purchase decision easily as well as it can help online sellers sell any kinds of products from internet easily.

In behavioral economic view, technology can change human behavior to be improved, it can let human feels comfortable, more free time ro use, rapid making any decisions, such as apply smart phones to make share purchase or sale transaction decision, online shopping decision, even travelling any where decision in short time, when the traveller finds the most cheap hotel accommodation room price and air ticket price frm any travel agent online tourism webstore, then the potential travel customer can follow the online hotel accommodation price and air ticket price data to make decision when to buy the air ticket from the airline travel agent or make decision when to prebook which hotel accommodation room to go to the country to travel from online travel agent tourism webstores. So, technology can encourage global any country travelers to make anywhere to trvel rapidly. If the traveler can find the country's general hotel rooms and airline tickets prices had been decreasing more sightly. The traveler may make travel decision to choose the country to travel in short time, then he/she can prebook the country;s any hotel room and airline ticket to pay by visa fraom the country's any hotel and airline travel agent webstores., before one week, even one month or more easily. Hence, online technology can also encourage traveler individual frequent travel times to be increased, due to global travelers can find any hotel rooms and airline tickets prices from internet conveniently at homes. They do not need to spend time to visit any airline travel agent to enquire travel choice country's hotel rooms prices and airline ticket prices. They can compare global travel of countries choices ' all hotels rooms and airline agents air tickets prices to make prebook airline seat and hotel room decision before one week, one month even six months early.

On conclusion, online technology can encourage global travelers can make travelling any where and when traveling time desicions easily. It can excite tourism industry develops in long time. Also, such as electricity cars invention can encourage environment protection car owners do car purchase decision easily, because they can choose to drive electronic energy cars to replace oil energy cars in order to avoid air pollution occurs easily. So, electronic cars can increase electronic car purchasrs number, due to many of environmental protection attitude of car owners can choose to drive electricity cars to bring air cleans, even non -manual driving cars can encourage lazy driving and free time driving car owners to choose to buy non-manual (artificial intelligent) cars to drive , because they can spend much free time to read, listen music or do any matters in themselves cars, they do not need to drive cars, robotic (AI) auto driving machine is such one non-manual driver to help them to drive themselves cars confidently. So, non-manual driving cars can attract lazy and enjoying free time driving car owners to choose to buy to replace traditional manual cars to drive easily. Moreover, online share transaction can help any share investors to make share buying and selling decision in short time easily. When they can apply smart phones technological tool to carry on share buying and selling activities easily. They can observe any share rising or falling price suitation from smart phones in any where any any time easily. So, smart phone technology can help global any shareholders to make share purchase and sale transaction easily. So, technology can encourage human makes decision in short time rapidly.

How and why employees behaviors may influence economy development?

In behavioral economy view,I believe the country's any organizational employees behavior may bring indirect relationship to influence the country's long term economic development. I shall indicate past manufacture industry social development period to explain their relationship. For many countries' past business activities had belonged to manufacturing industry, such as US, UK past before 1980 year, it focused on steel manufacturing and steel manufacturing related machine products. So, US, Uk developed countries manufacturing industries may be past main country's economic income sources. I assume US , UK past had one million number different kinds of industries. They ought had about seven houndred thousand number organizational businesses were belonged to manufactured industry. They may include:

Steel manufacturing and steel related machine manufacturing, e.g. vehicle manufacturing, home appliances, e.g. washing machine, television, radio, refrigerate cooler, heater, air condition etc. different kinds of different kinds of steel -related manufacturing machine, they were manufactured from US, UK steel machine manufacturers. So, US, Uk the other three hundred thousand number industry may be general service industry, e.g. hotel service, restaurent, cinema, public transport service, tourism lesiure , wine bar, supermarket etc. different kinds of non-manufacturing industries business organizations were operated in UK, US past before 1980 year.

So, in UK, US developed countries industry development history, they ought have high percentage of businesses belonged to steel related manufacturing machine and steel products. Also, in the past before 1980 year, US, Uk business employers , they employed many workers are manufacturing workers. They needed to spend long time to work in factories. They were skillful workers, and they are trained to manufacturing cars, washing machine, television, heater, etc. even steel itself different kinds of steel related products to prepare to deliver to their shops to sell to US, Uk local or overseas clients.

So, I believe that past UK, US ought employ many employees, they belonged to skillful manufacturing workers, manufacture increasing steel machine or steel related machine number of products rapidly daily. So, if UK, US had had many of these manufacturing factories owned high skillful workers, then their manufacturing steel-related machine or steel both kinds of products number must be influenced to raise rapidly. Consequently, their steel machine manufacturing products would been exported to overseas or would been sold to local both markets , they may be influenced to raise sale number. They (these manufacturing workers) needed to be trained to know how to manufactur these different kinds of machine products in the efficient teams and they ought to be trained to raise their efficiencies in order to shorten time to manufacturing many kinds of steel related manufacturing machine or steel itself products rapidly. So , if their efficiencies and manufacturing performance was improved, these US, UK any one manufacturing worker and their teams ought achieve raising productivities significantly.

Hence, when past UK, US manufacturing industry development period, if these two countries' any manufacturing factories could have many manufacturing workers could be trained to be skillful and proficient manufacturing workers. Then, in past every day to these factories workers, they ought help their steel or steel related manufacturing employers to raise any kinds of machine or steel products number in every team. So, when past in the manufacturing industry development, US, UK could have many factories' manufacturing workers themselves steel or steel related machine products manufacturing skill could be trained to to improve to any kinds of these machine or steel manufacuring products quality as well as their products number could be influenced to raise by themselves skillful improvement significantly every day.

Then, what would be influenced to occur to past UK, US manufacturing industry period? In behavioral economic view, when these two manufacturing industry developed countries, such as UK, US , if they had many factories workers can be trained to improve their skill in order to achieve any kinds of steel or steel-related machine products quality could be improved as well as products manufacturing number could be also increased absolutely.

In consequence, past UK and US both countries ought increase themselves any kinds of steel and steel related machine products number to be supplied to themselves local shops to let local clients to choose any one kind of machine manufacturing products to buy easily as well as they could also export to supply overseas any countries to buy their different kinds of steel or steel related machine products to let overseas steel or steel related manufacturing machine product buyers, they can have many of these different kinds of these steel or steel-related different kinds of manufacturing machine from UK and UK these both countries easily to compare other countries.

On conclusion, I believe that past US, and UK macro manufacturing industry income GDP would increase significantly. So, they would have good economic growth performance because when many of these manufacturing workers themselves manufacturing effort could be improved. So, it explained when employees manufacturing abilities can influence economic growth indirectly.

Robots invention whether they can help organizations to raise efficiencies or inefficiencies?

In behavioral economic view, in any organizations, when the organization hopes its worker teams can raise efficiencies , the organization may choose to increase more workers number and/or it can provide training to improve these workets themselves skills in order to raise their efficiencies. For one warehouse example, when the warehouse increases many goods , they are needed to delivered these goods from the shelves to the delivering destination locations. If this warehouse supervisors feel these workers themselves goods delivery speeds are slow, which is possible due to this warehouse's workers number is not enough. So, this warehouse supervisor ought increase workers number in order to increase their goods delivery speed in order to deliver goods from the shelves to every indicated goods delivery destination in order to let any one lorry driver can transport the right kinds of goods and ensure the accurate goods number to transport to any one client home rapidly.

However, if this warehouse supervisor planed to buy several warehouse goods delivery robots to assist these warehouse workers to find the right kinds of goods from shelves and then deliver to the right destination location in the warehouse. So, these warehouse orkers can concentrate on counting the accurate goods number and ensuring the right kinds of goods in order to prepare to let lorry drivers to transport these goods to these goods of buyers themselvers homes rapidly. Consequently, in the first step, robots can concentrate on finding th right goods from shelves and delivers them to the right goods transportation of location destination. Then, in the second step, these warehouse workers can concentrate on counting the accurate goods number and ensuring the right kinds of goods in order to prepare to put them to the lorry. Consequently, when warehouse robots and warehouse workers can cooperate to work together, the most important, robots, can deal on finding the right kinds of goods and deal on delivering the accurate number of goods of job duty as well as these warehouse workers can only concentrte on counting the right kinds of goods number in order to avoid it has none any mistake of wrong kinds of goods and inaccurate goods of delivery number to be transported to the lorry and to deliver to any one buyer's home.

So, it seems that warehouse robots ought help any one warehouse worker to raise himself efficiency and avoid goods delivery of mistake occurrence easily as well as their help to warehouse workers that can let any one goods buyer feels their goods can be delivered to their homes rapidly. Moreover, warehouse robots can also help these warehouse workers to raise efficiencies because warehouse robots can help them to shorten goods delivery time between any one shelf and any one goods delivery destination of location in the warehuse because robots may help them to find the right kinds of goods from the right shelf in the short time. So, any one worker does not need to spend long time to seek anywhere is the right shelf location for the kind of goods when the kind of goods are needed to deliver to the buyer's home from lorry. Warehouse robots can help them to do this aspect of " finding the goods from the right shelf in short time job duty". So, any one warehouse worker only needed tospend less time to do the counting of any right kind of goods number and ensuring the right kind of goods job duty. Consequently, this warehouse 's any one worker, his any one kind of goods delivery time may be reduced, because robots' assistance and they may have more confidence to avoid mistake to deliver the wrong number of goods and/or the wrong kind of goods to any one goods buyer's home.

On conclusion, it seems that warehouse robots ought may help any one warehouse worker to raise efficiency for any one team in the warehouse as well as the warehouse any one supervisor does not need to spend much time to observe any one worker individual performance for " goods delivery job duty aspect" because their goods delivery job duty that had been replaced to do by these several warehouse robots. Robots can achieve the more accurate of right kinds of goods and the right number of goods delviery job performance to compare any one of human warehouse worker themselves right kinds of goods of delivery and right number of goods of delivery job performance. So, when robots can participate to cooperate with this warehouse's any one worker to do their goods of delivery job duty in this warehouse every day. Then, robots can raies any one of supervisor individual confidence in order to let they do not need to spend time to observe any one of worker individual whose goods of delivery job performane. They can concentrate on supervising any one worker whose goods transport to lorry in the final step in order to avoid to deliver wrong goods number and / or wrong kind of goods to any one goods buyer's home every day. Consequently, this warehouse's overall teams of their delviery of goods performance many be improved by robotss' participatin to goods of delivery task as well as this warehouse's oveall teams themselves efficiencies may be influenced to raise by robots' goods of delivery task participation.

Why social behavior may influence organizational strategy needs to be changed ?

Why any organizations need to know whether nowadays social behaivor how has been changing in order to implement the kind of the most right strategy to achieve the profit aim pursue in possible. I shall indicate nowadays ecommerce or online, customer shopping behavior to explain above question concerns they ought have close relationship between social behavior and organizational strategic choice or organizational behavioral changing need.

On nowadays ecommerce business, or online shopping model, this kind of shopping model in global many young and old age consumers like to apply internet tool to choose any country sellers website stores in order to stay at home to buy any kinds of products from themselves webstores in global societies.

In fact, online shopping model had been popular for long time above to twenty years. Most of global sellers will make decision to design themselves webstores in order to attract global many online buyers to choose to buy their products from themselves webstores. So, it seems that social consumers purchase behaviors had been changed to online shopping from internet invention.

Hence, social consumers purchase behavioral changes may influence any organizations' strategies need to be changed from visiting shops purchase strategy model to online purchase strategy model, if the seller still concentrate on concentrate on considerate how to design itelf , but neglects to considerate how to design itself webstore, e.g. how to design attract product photos to put on itself webstore, how to arrange sale price information location to be putted on webstore and visa card payment location on itself webstore in order to let any one online buyer can feel very easier to buy itself any kinds of products from itself webstore. Then, its potential online buyers will be influenced to increase number when they can find this online seller itself any kinds of products photes and every kinds of product sale price information and visa card payment channel locations easily from itself webstore.

So, it implies that nowadays any one seller ought need to design one webstore to let any one online overseas and domestic consumers can have chance to click itself webstore to choose any one kind of product to buy conveniently when he/she does not hope to leave him/her home to go to shop, because nowadays social shopping behaviors had been influenced to change when internet invention, them it gives another online purchase method to replace visiting shops purchase method to global any one buyer in nowadays societies.

So, if nowadays any one seller still concentrate on how to design itself shop display in order to put any kinds of product on shelf in order to let any one visiting shop customer to find the kind of product to buy, but it neglects to change to choose to pursue another new technological shopping method, such as webstore purchase method in order to implement effective strategy to design the most right webstore as well as in order to attract global overseas and local consumers to find itself webstore easily from website and find its any one kind of product phots and sale price and visa card payment button in order to choose to buy itself any kinds of products in the short time. Consequently I believe that the seller will lose many customers from overseas and local when its other same or similar product sellers choose to design themselves webstores in order to let global any one product buyer can buy themselves any one kind of product when they can pay visa card to buy their products from them webstores conveniently when they stay at home habitly. Then, the seller will lose many global potential customers in long time.

On conclusion, in behavioral economic view, any consumer behavioral social changing, which will influence any in order to avoid customers number loses significantly . In future time, organizations need to make rapid decision in order to implement the most reasonable and the most useful strategy in order to avoid global potential customers number reduces or lose them in long time. So, social behavioral changing environment ought influence any global organizations need to decide how to change themselves strategies in order to avoid customers loses significantly in future time.

How and why human behavior may influence economic growth or recession?

May ourselves daily behaviors influence our global societial continue economic growth or recession? Do they have cause and effect close relationship between human behaviors and global economic growth or recession? I shall apply behavioral economic theory to analyze and explain whether ourselves daily behaviors and our global societial economic growth

or recession which have close cause and effect relationship as below:
Every country itself economic development must depend on any business activities, otherwise, any kinds of business activities must need ourselves business activities or behaviors in order to achieve any business activities as well as achieve the country's overall economic development in macro view. However, any country's overall business activites or behaviors which must depend on any kinds of individual businessmen, themselves employees daily working behavior or activity or performance in order to help them to attract or increase many clients number to acieve " earning profit" aim. So, it seems that any individual business, itself overall every department individual working behavior is one main factor to influence the company's overall business performance.

For agricultural fruit and meat food farming industry example, such as New Zealand is a farming main target industry country. It had had many New Zealanders were daily themselves own farming businesses for many years. Their farming businesses include growing fruit, sheep, cow, pig pork, meat etc. food sale business. If the New Zealand farmer owned a large size farming land, then he will choose either growing fruit or feeding sheeps, pigs, cows to be meat to to transport to New Zealand supermarkets to help them to sell to their farmers meet to New Zealanders in order to earn profit. Thus, if the New Zealand farmer owned large size of farming lands, then he needs to employ many farming employees (farming workers) to help him to carry on farming business daily tasks, e.g. picking up friuts, feeding pigs, cows, sheeps to eat food daily. These daily farming jobs are very important to influence this New Zealand farmer's meats or fruits sale number whether they can be easy or diffcult to sell in New Zealand supermarkets , if these farming workers can own encough farming knowledge or skill to know how to pick up fruits method and make judgement to know whether it is right time to pick up the kind of fruits from the trees , as well as know how feed this pigs, sheeps, cows to eat food in order to let they are better health. Consequently, their farming behaviors which can let these animals can provide the best taste and enough meat from these animals to let New Zealander to buy to eat from New Zealand any one supermarket. Even these New Zealand farming workers can know whether the kinds of fruits, e.g. oranges, apples, gapes etc. fruits whether they ought be picked up from the trees at the right time. Consequently, they can make judgement to decide to pick up any kinds of the best taste fruits to let any one New Zealander to buy to eat from any one supermarket in New Zealand. Otherwise, if they do not make judegement to know whether the kind of fruit ought not be picked up because they still need longer time to continue grow up to increase fruit size and better taste from the trees in order to let any one fruit buyer can feel better taste when they eat this kind of fruit later. If they can buy this kind of fruit to eat later, then this New Zealand farmer's his fruit buyers can buy the best taste of this kind of fruit to eat from an yone supermarket in New Zealand. Consequently, many New Zealand supermarkets will choose to buy any kinds of fruits from this farmer fruit supplier when they feel this farmer's fruits can provide more better taste fruits to compare other farmers' fruits.

Thus, due to New Zealand is one farming main income source country. It's any kinds of fruits and meats need to be export to overseas to sell , instead of local sale. It's GDP percent is very high to whole country 's overall income source. So, any one New Zealand farmer individual and any one farming worker individual working behavior will influence its economy whether it is influenced to grow or recession possible. Moreover, it also seems that farming workers' farming knowledge and skill will influence themselves farming daily activities to achieve the aim of the number of increase or decrease to any kinds of fruits whether they are better taste or the number of increase of decrease to any kinds of meats whether they are better taste to supply to any one New Zealand fruit or meat buyers to eat from any one New Zealand supermarket. So, it implies that any one New Zealand farming worker individual farming behavior may influence any kinds of fruits or any kinds of meat taste because they are transported to any one supermarket to sell in New Zealand.

Consequently, if New Zealans had many farmers can teach god farming knowledge and skill to let their any one farming workers know how to decide judgement to decide when it is right time to pick up any kinds of fruits from trees , or how to grow them on soil in order to let they can grow rapidly. Then, many different kinds of fruits can be provided to let any one New Zealanders can eat the best taste of fruits when their fruits are supplied to any one New Zealand supermarkets. Even, if they knew how to feed foods to pigs, cows, sheeps to eat daily. Then they can be more health and they can provide the best taste of meats to let any one New Zealanders can buy their meats from any one New Zealand supermarkets. Moreover, their fruits and meats can be transported to overseas to let any one country fruits or meats buyers can choose any kinds of New Zealand meats and fruits to buy to eat from themselves countries supermarkets. Then, many overseas fruit and meat buyers will perfer to choose New Zealand any kinds of fruits or meats to buy to compare other countries fruits or meats to buy when they go to any one local supermarkets.

On conclusion, it seems that New Zealand farming workers themselves farming behavior may influence their farming employers any kinds of fruits or meats sale number and income because their farming task behaviors must influence whether their fruits or meats taste are the better taste or worse taste to compare their other local farmers (the farmer competitors) whose fruits or meats taste. If tthe farmer's any one farming worker can be trained to learn how to know to feed animals skill and when is the most right time to pick up any kinds of fruits from trees or how to grow them on the soil methods. Due to these farming worker individual farming behavior may influence his different finds of fruits and meats sale number to be increase or decrease, so these any one New Zealand farmer must need to depend on any one farming worker whose farming working methods, if their farming working behaviors can be the best to influence any kinds of fruits to grow rapid or any kinds of pigs, cows, sheeps animals grow up rapidly , then their sale number may be increase significantly and their taste can be improved to let any New Zealand or overseas meat or fruit buyer to buy to eat to feel from any one New Zealand or overseas supermarkets, then New Zealand's agriculture industry must be influenced to increase. In the world, any one fruit or meat buyer must choose to buy New Zealand's fruit and meat to eat in prefer to compare other countries' fruits and meats. So, New Zealand's GDP may be influenced to raise from any one New Zealand farming worker individual farming working behaviors.

Reasons why human behavior may influence economic recession or growth?

Can ourselves daily behaviors or activies influence ourselves countries' economic growth or recession? I shall attempt to explain the reasons why they have direct or indirect relationship between human behavior and economy growth or recession as below:

I shall indicate environment pollution case to attempt to explain above question. Our societies had been experiencing servious environment pollution challenge. However, environment pollution , such as air pollution is caused by air planes and vehicles emission by air planes and vehicles emission as well as water pollution is caused by plastic rubblish, or dirty water or oil or gas chemical material, these both kinds of pollution ought may bring economic recession and this both kinds of pollution are caused by human ourselves daily foolish activities.

I believe human behavior and economy and pollution which have cause and effect relationship. I shall analyze this environment pollution case to explain why they have case and effect relationship between human foolish behavior and environment pollution and economic recession as below:

When global societies had many people like to buy cars to drive to bring emission to fresh air on the roads as well as many manufacturing factories will bring emission to pollute fresh air in their manufacturing processes. Factories and cars will bring air pollution , due to factories need to pollute fresh air in order to manufacture many products and car owners need to drive their cars to go to offices or leisure places. Their cars will also bring emisson to pollute fresh air. On consequence, car owners themselves frequent driving behaviors and factory workers themselves frequent manufacturing behaviors may bring environment pollution. Technology or human behavior whether may influence economic growth or recession. Moreover, air planes also brings emission to pollute air when they are flying in sky. Also, when ships bring oil pollution or sea plastic rubblishs bring pollution to global oceans.

In fact, manufactuers and cars owners, such as factories workers manufacturing behaviours ans car owners driving behaviors and pilots driving air planes flying behaviors and ships transport behaviors, which may cause plastic rubblish, oil or gas emission to sky or sea or on the road to cause ocean and air pollution is serious. However, human ourselves need to buy cars to drive to satisfy ourselves driving leisure or enjoyment, travelers need to catch air planes to travel to enjoy leisure needs, factories workers need help factories to manufacture many products to sell to customers to satisfy their using needs. oil exploration needs to find lands to explore new oil lands.

All of these business and leisure activites may bring serious air and water pollution. However, due to serious air and water pollution will bring earth warming challenge , such as some countries temperature will be influences to rise up to 40 degree or higher br earth warming. However, earth warming is caused by air and ocean pollution. Pollution must be caused by human ourselves, driving cars leisure and factories manufacturing business activities. Hence, if human decided to continue to do these foolish behaviors, we only pursue to manufacture different kinds of industrial products or drive cars to enjoy leisure aims, but we also neglect ourselves behaviors may bring environment pollution. Then, earth warming or earth temperature will be influenced to rise up absolutely in long term. Moreover, if our future earth will be influenced to bring serious high temperature effect by human ourselves these foolish behaviors.

On consequencey, warth warming will bring serious economic losses in possible because when ourselves earth temperature had been influenced to rise up to 40 degree or high. Ourselves health will be caused poor, due to we will feel difficult breath, we must need often tried and hard to work, due to our nervous and health will be influenced to poor by pollution and earth warming effect. Also, we need to pay more money to see doctors when we had long life. Then, our societies will lose may strong labors to help manufacturers to work, e.g. factories will reduce workers number to help manufacturers to produce more different kinds of products, due to workers health is general poor. Due to lacking enough workers to manufacture products, our societies will begin to reduce enough supply number of products to sell to global consumers to satisfy their use needs.

On conclusion, in behaviroal economic view, our societies will lose many labors due to their bodies are not health by air and water pollution. Global economic and business activities will be influenced to worse by global workers reducing number reason. So, economic recession will begin to occur in possible when pollution reaches the serious level.

How employee behavior influences organizational development?

Can any organizational department employee individual behavior may help the organization to bring long term development? When one employee individual behavior, manager won't feel whose task behavior may help organizational development, but when the department has many teams cooperate to work together , all of these team employees whose task behaviors may help their organization to bring long term development.

I shall explain how any why when the organization has many departments, as well as when every team memmber individual behavior may help whole organization to bring long term development in possible as below:

Every organization must need efficient department to cooperate to work together. They may include human resource, finance, logistic, facility management, sales, marketing , operateional , warehouse , factory manufacture , research and development, purchase, customer service etc. different kinds of departments to cooperate to work together. So, any one employee individual behavior, include manager, leader, supervisor, worker, salesperson, manufacture worker, adminisration staff, factory or logistic worker etc. themselves task behavior whether his/her performance is worse or better , whose task behavior ought bring long term good or bad influence to cause the organization's whose efficiency, or performance , whether it can be influenced to improve significantly. For car factory manufacture workers department example, it exmploys 100 car manufacturing workers. They need to manufacture at least 50 cars in order to bring enough car manufacture number to supply to global car buyers to choose to buy (satisfaction to car buyers their driving leisure activity needs). However, if this car manufacture firm employs many low skilful car manufacture workers, their inefficient car skill may bring cars manufacture number reduces, they can not achieve to reach the at least 50 cars manufacture number, if these 100 car manufacture workers. They have half number of workers, they only manufacture 30 to 40 cars number at least daily. So, it seems that this car manufacture firm will have half car manufacture workers bring the low cars manufacture number to compare the another half cars manufacture workers, when this proficient car manufacture workers may manufacture at least 60 or more cars manufacture number daily. So, it explains that this inefficient car manufacture workers will not help this car manufacture company to manufacture enough cars number in order to supply to global car market to sell to satisfy global car buyers needs, when car buyers demand number is more thn car manufacture supply number in supply and demand view. Hence, in long term, if this car manufacture company can not employ new proficient car manufacture workers to replace those inefficient or low skillful car workers. Consequently, its car manufacture number must be influenced to reduce and it can not satisfy global car buyers driving leisure needs.

However, if this car manufacture firm also has shop to sell itself any kinds of cars, instead of manufacturing cars product. So, it needs have both main departments to help it to earn profit. The first step, it needs have proficient car manufacture workers to help it to manufacture at least 50 cars from every car worker in order to have enough cars number to be provided to global car sellers to help it to sell to global car customers. Second step, if it decided to attempt to sell itself cars. Then, it needs to set up car shops in global to different countries in order to let global car buyers may visit its global any one car shop to enquire any one car etc. salesperson about any car quality, speed, gas useful, price, safety, etc. information questions and they can attempt to sit in any one car to feel whether which car can let them to feel more comfortable to make final car purchase decision in any one shop. So, if this car company can provide good sale speaking skillful training to any one car salesperson to let his/her to know whether how to explain every kind of car function and feature, manufacture method etc. questions, then I believe that they can influence any one car buyer to makecar purchase choice decision more easily. So, it this car manufacturer hopes it may attempt to earn profit from different countries car sellers and car buyers both. It ought also provide training course to all general car salespeople to be proficient owning sale speaking skillful professional skill in order to prepare having more confidence to persuade any one car customer to make car purchase choice from any one car salesperson more easily to compare global other car sellers.

Hence, if this car manufacturer could build both car manufacturing team and car sale team more proficient. However, if this car manufacturer hopes to develop itself car manufacture busness to expend to car sale business both in success. It must need to spend long term to provide training courses to general car manufacture workers and general car salespeople both to be proficient car skillful manufacture workers and proficient car skillful salespeople in order to help they can manufacture enough car numbers and help they can persuade may car customers can make car purchase decision in short time when they visit its any one car shop.

However, this car manufacture company explains why every car manufacture worker whose manufacturing behavior and every car salesperson sale persuading speaking ability may help this car manufacture company to expand from its car manufacture market to car sale market development in sussess in possible. So, this car manufacture firm must need these two kinds of essential human resource elements in order to achieve its cars sale number and cars manufacture number increasing aim. They may include proficient car manufacture workers and proficient car salespeople both human resource elements. These both human resource daily task behavior may influence its long term task efficient performance in order to expand itself car sale business in success from itself car manufacture business easily. If it hopes to expand its car manufacture business to car sale business in success. It must need to provide training to these two departments general staffs to be proficient staffs in order to supply enough cars number to its global car shops to let global car buyers can choose its any kinds of cars to buy in any time.

Morevoer, if this car manufacture company can have good skillful of car research and development department , it aims to research and innovate any new technological cars invention in order to improve its any traditional old kinds of cars to be innovative new kinds of cars from every year. Consequently, its any new innovative cars ought attract global any one car buyer to make car purchase choice final decision more easily, because its any kinds of manufacturng cars can be innovated rapidly to compare its any one car manufacturing competitors, when its nay kinds of cars can be shorten time to innovate within three months, but its any one car manufacturing competitors need to spend more than three months, even one year to innovate themselves traditional old cars products in long term. Hence, its car staffs research and development department staffs must need own good car product design ability, proficient car engineering knowledge , even car invention knowledge in order to innovate its any one kind of car product in short time and introduce to let its global car proficient car buyers feel surprise to its any one kind of innovative car products to compare its any one car manufacturer.Hence, these four departments: car manufacture, car sale and car research and development anr car training departments must need concentrate resource to provide enough training to any one staffs in order to achieve the best performance.

On conclusion, all these departments staffs their performance can influence car manufacture aim to chance to car manufacture and sale aim more significantly. it explains why some main department staffs whole behaviors may influence any organizational performance significantly.

Artificial intelligent Human clever and art creating ability methods

How robots create human clever and art creating ability? Nowadays robots invention may help businesses to reduce employees number, improve performance, raise productivities, reduce cost in service industry,manufacturing industry, office , warehouse, restaurant, hotel , factory, cinema etc. different kinds of business environments, even public transport tools. However, instead of robots may bring these above advantages to any kinds of business working and service environments, whether robots may also help human to create clever and image creating ability. I shall attempt to answer this question:

On the one hand, I believe that past technology ,e.g. machine , it should not have ability to help human to create clever and image creative ability,but nowadays, robots invention that I believe it had had enough ability to help future human to raise more clever and more creating image or painting picture, art design etr. image ability, after robots had been experienced above more than ten years improvement stage from early research stage to invention stage, till to nowadays improvement stage, e.g. non-manual driving auto vehicels, even future non-manual driving skill may be improved to apply to public transport tools, e.g. trams, trains,buses, airplanes, ships etc. public transport tools, when non-manual driving skills can be improved to own the most safe driving skillful ability to compare human driving skills.

On another hand, when robots could be invented to be applied to medical or hospital surgery aspect, e.g. roboting surgerys may help surgery doctors to do complex surgery in surgery rooms, or serving patients tasks in any hospital working environments. They can help nurses and doctors to spend more time to do more important tasks urgently, so medical or surgery serving robots may help nurses and surgery doctors to reduce task load pressure and create clever or improve their surgery skills to when they can cooperate to work in hospitals.

On the other hand, robots can be invented to help any public transport drivers to avoid more traffic accidents occurrence on any countries roads. So, it seems that non-manual driving public transport tools invention may also help human drivers to improve driving skills in possible, when they can learn how to avoid sudden traffic accidents occurrence in any countries roads in any time. so, any kindsof public transport tool drivers ought learn how to avoid traffic accidents skills from future non-manual driving robots invention. Instead of non-manual driving robots and hospital patients medical care or surgery service robots may help public transport tools drivers and hospital nurses and doctors to concentrate on spending time to treat any more important and urgent matters every days. Even, future restaurants may let cooking restaurants may let cooking robots to help human cookers to cook more different kinds of good taste food, to human cookers may learn cooking robots cooking skills in order to improve themselves traditional cooking skills often, in order to compare their cooking skills between human cookers and cooking robots.

On conclusion, it seems that cooking robots ought help human cookers to create any kinds of new cooking skills. Moremove, futuer robot cookers ought be future human cookers their cooking coaches. These robot cookers will help human cookers to create clever cooking skills in possible. Also, future non-manual driving robots ought help human drivers to create new driving skills in order to improve their driving skills to reduce sudden traffic accidents occurrence easily on any countries roads in any time, future hospital surgery or patient care service robots may help surgeons or nurses to do any surgerys in surgery rooms or looking care patients in hospitals. So, when robot surgeons help human surgeons to do complex surgerys in surgerical rooms, human surgeons can learn how to do more complex surgerical tasks for every surgeons when human surgeons can observate every surgerical robots how to do surgeons together. Hence, it seems that robot surgeons also may create future human surgeons themselves innovate surgerical skills from traditional surgerical skills improvement. So, future artificial intelligent technology ought help any kinds of human occupations to create clever, even improvement themselves traditional skills to new innovative skills absolutely.

Why does technology raise online products sale demand and reduces shops products sale demand?

Nowadays robot technology is popular to be applied to different aspects of our daily lives. They may include: non-manual driving vehicles, smart phones, space rockets, kitchen cookers, shopping centres service, cinema ticket sale, etc. different kinds of businesses demand. However, instead of internet invention may influence global communication, media channel is changed to computer internet, media channel is changed to computer internet, media communication from traditional newspaper, letter, TV, radio etc. communication channel. So, any internet users may click to yahoo.com news website to read global news from computer yahoo.com website easily.

In fact, internet technology is also used from businesses. They attempt to set up themselves web stores to sell their products from themselves webstores. So, any one product buyers may buy any kinds of products from any one webstores when they stay at homes. It is very convenient and common to future any one webstore shoppers. It brings this question: Can webstores help online product purchases needs raise and influence shop product purchases need reduce?

In demand and supply view, when one product price raises, its sale demand ought reduce, unless, it can attract to influence customers need consideration or its supply number decreases. But, when one product is increasing sale price to seel from the seller's webstore, whether its sale number will be influenced to reduce. Also, when the kind of product is selling and its sale price is raised, whether it can still keep demand number increase as well as whether it can influence its similar kinds of competitor their products sale demand number to reduce from shop sale channel.

In demand and supply view, when one product price raises, its sale demand ought reduce, unless, it can attract to influence customers need consideration or its supply number decreases. But when one product is increasing sale price to sell from the seller's webstore, whether its sale number will be influenced to reduce. Also, when the kind of product is selling and its sale price is raised, whether it can still keep demand number increases as well as whether it can influence its similar kinds of competitors their products sale demand number to reduce from shop sale channel.

I suppose that webstore sale may influence shop sale demand number decreases, because when internet is popular to use, when one country's buyer wants to buy one kind of product, but he/she can not find the kind of product can be bought from himself/herself home country. If he/she can findthe kind of product to buy from any one of overseas webstore from internet channel at home in any time. Then, he/she will be influenced to make purchase decision from the seller's websote immediately. So, it implies that when on consumer plans to buy one kind of product, he / she will attempt to find the kind of product from any one seller's webstore in preferat home, if he/she spend long time to find the kind of product from many of webstores, but he /she still does not find the kind of product from many of webstores, then he/she will choose to visit any one shop to attempt to buy the kind of product.Hence, online shopping purchase channel will be prefer choice to compare visiting shopd purchase channel in nowadays society.

So, it explains that why the kind of product online sale number may influence the kind of similar product visiting shop sale number either increases or decreases. It means that the kind of product visiting shops sale number may still increases , if the kind of similar products supply number is not enough , they are difficult to let any one online buyer to find to buy from any one webstore. Otherwise, if the kind of similar products sale supply number is enough to let any one online buyer to find from many webstores. Then, they can influence the similar kinds of shop products purchase demand to reduce and their shops purchase demand will be also influenced to reduce from webstores purchase channel.

On conclusion, it explains that the kind of shop products demand number ought be influenced to increase or decrease, when the similar kind of products can be bought easily from many webstores from internet (e-commerce) shopping channel. Internet (online) technology may help the seller to raise the kind of product competitive ability on purchase demand aspect, when there are not many other sellers can provide webstores to sell the similar kind of products and they only concentrate on selling the kind of similar products from shops to let any one online buyer to frind from may webstores. Then, they can influence the similar kinds of shop products purchase demand to reduce and their shops purchase demand will be also influenced to reduce from webstores purchase channel. Hence, webstore and shop both purchase channel explains that the similar kinds of shop products demand number will be influenced to increase or decrease , when the kinds of product can be bought easily from many webstores from internet shopping channel. Internet technology may help the seller to raise the kind of product competitive abilty to raise purchase demand when there are not many other sellers can provide webstores to sell the kind of similar products and they only concentrate on selling the kind of similar products from shops.

Does car technological development reach mature stage to help economic development?

Our societies had been developing too many years. In our past technological aspect, machine invention had began till to computer invention till to internet invention. It seems that our technological development stage may reach mature stage. Why do I feel our technological development had reached mature stage. I shall apply demand and supply economic theory to explain this question as below:

I shall indicate car development industry to explain whether when car development stage can reach mature stage, it may help global economic growth. In our car technological development stage, it is from gas energy car invention till to nowadays battery energy car invention till to even future non-manual driving car invention. Do you feel that when human (car buyers) felt environmental protecion need to avoid air pollution. So, battery energy cars demand number may increase , it will influence gas energy cars demand number reduces. Even, if future non0manula driving cars invention succeed, lazy driving car buyers will choose to buy non-manual driving (robot driving cars) in preference. So, it is possible that , it will influence future gas energy cars demand number reduces much. I mean that when car buyers can choose many different kinds of non-manual driving cars and battery energy cars to buy. Then, gas energy cars demand number must be influenced to reduce very much as well as gas energy cars supply number will be influenced to reduce to avoid sale prices reduce.

Hence, it explains why future car technological development will reach mature stage when both kinds of non-manual driving cars and battery energy cars are invented to the mature stage. When these two kinds of cars invention can satisfy future global car buyers driving needs. Then, car maufacturers won't need to spend too much time to continue to attempt to invent any new kinds of cars in order to excite future car buyers' purchase decision. So, I believe that car technological development will reach mature stage within five years, if non-manual driving cars and battery energy cars are invented in success and they can be popular to accept to drive to global car buyers.

On conclusion, when car technological development reaches matural stage, it will help future economy continue grows because when car manufacturers had invented many new kinds of non-manual driving cars and new kinds of non-manual driving cars and new battery energy car sale market. Then, they will encourage or attract global many car buyers choose to buy these both kinds of cars products in preference to compare to traditional gas energy car products. So, they will influence many traditional gas- energy car buyers forgive to drive gas energy cars to avoid non pollution and lazy driving behavioral feeling. So, gas energy car reselling number will increase between gas energy car drivers and past non-owning any car buyers. Also, non-manual driving cars and battery energy car supplying number will be influenced to increase when battery energy car buyers and non-manual driving car buyers driving needs increase.

Consequently, these factors will influence global gas energy cars, non-manual driving cars and battery energy cars their cars purchase and sale transactions increase in future global car market. So, I believe that global car technological development could reach matural stage, then it will infuence global car buyers number increases as well as this car technological mature development stage may also bring global rapid economic growth future non-manual driving car buyers and battery energy car buyers both number increases.

On conclusion, due to nowadays technology is needed to continue to develop in order to invent any kinds of new products to satisfy consumer individual need , even job market need, even future space tourism leisure need. So, I believe that technology development may influence future space tourism continue development in order to satisfy future space traveler individual leisure need.